ACTIVITY & TEST PREP WORKBOOK

SIDE by SIDE

THIRD EDITION

BOOK 2

Steven J. Molinsky • Bill Bliss

with

Carolyn Graham • Peter S. Bliss

Contributing Authors

Dorothy Lynde • Elizabeth Handley

Illustrated by

Richard E. Hill

TO THE TEACHER

This enhanced edition of *Side by Side Activity Workbook 2* includes practice tests designed to prepare students for the types of standardized tests and performance assessments used by many instructional programs to measure and report students' progress. A practice test for each chapter of the series simultaneously assesses students' achievement of the chapter's instructional objectives, provides intensified coverage of lifeskill competencies, and prepares students for standardized general language proficiency tests that assess students' educational advancement and reflect programs' effectiveness in meeting outcome-based performance standards.

The practice tests appear in the second section of this workbook on pages T1–T58. They include: multiple-choice questions that assess vocabulary, grammar, reading, listening skills, lifeskill competencies, and basic literacy tasks (such as reading medicine labels, signs, and everyday documents); writing assessments that can be evaluated using a standardized scoring rubric and collected in portfolios of students' work; and speaking performance assessments designed to stimulate face-to-face interactions between students, for evaluation by the teacher using a standardized scoring rubric, or for self-evaluation by students.

Pages are perforated so that completed tests can be handed in and can serve as a record of students' participation and progress in the instructional program. Scripts for the listening assessment activities are included at the end of this volume and may be removed if desired. An accompanying teacher's volume, the *Side by Side Activity & Test Prep Workbook 2 Teacher's Resource Book*, includes answer keys, scoring rubrics and guidelines, reproducible learner assessment records for documenting students' progress, teaching suggestions, and test preparation techniques.

Side by Side, 3rd edition
Activity & Test Prep Workbook 2

Copyright © 2004 by Prentice Hall Regents
Addison Wesley Longman, Inc.
A Pearson Education Company.
All rights reserved.
No part of this publication may be reproduced, stored in a retrieval system, or transmitted in any form or by any means, electronic, mechanical, photocopying, recording, or otherwise, without the prior permission of the publisher.

Pearson Education, 10 Bank Street, White Plains, NY
10606

Editorial director: *Pam Fishman*
Vice president, director of design and production:
 Rhea Banker
Director of electronic production:
 Aliza Greenblatt
Production manager: *Ray Keating*
Director of manufacturing: *Patrice Fraccio*
Associate digital layout manager: *Paula Williams*
Associate art director: *Elizabeth Carlson*
Interior design: *Elizabeth Carlson, Wendy Wolf*
Cover design: *Elizabeth Carlson, Warren Fischbach*

The authors gratefully acknowledge the contribution of Tina Carver in the development of the original *Side by Side* program.

ISBN 0-13-040648-1

1 2 3 4 5 6 7 8 9 10 - CRK – 06 05 04 03

S0-AZQ-136

Contents

A WHAT DO THEY LIKE TO DO?

chat online	go hiking	go to the mall	play soccer	write letters
go dancing	go to the beach	listen to music	watch TV	

1. He _____ likes to _____

_____ watch TV _____ .

2. They _____

_____ .

3. She _____

_____ .

4. I _____

_____ .

5. They _____

_____ .

6. He _____

_____ .

7. She _____

_____ .

8. We _____

_____ .

9. My dog _____

_____ .

B LISTENING

Listen and choose the correct response.

1. a. He likes to chat online.
    b. They like to chat online.

2. a. I like to dance.
    b. She likes to dance.

3. a. He likes to read.
    b. She likes to read.

4. a. They like to play basketball.
    b. We like to play basketball.

5. a. He likes to go to the library.
    b. We like to go to the library.

6. a. You like to go to the mall.
    b. I like to go to the mall.

7. a. We like to play loud music.
    b. He likes to play loud music.

8. a. She likes to watch TV.
    b. They like to watch TV.

bake	go	listen	ride	sing	watch

1. Alan likes to _____ watch _____ TV.

   _____ He watches _____ TV every day.

   _____ He watched _____ TV yesterday.

   _____ He's going to watch _____ TV tomorrow.

2. I like to _____ to music.

   _____ to music every day.

   _____ to music yesterday.

   _____ to music tomorrow.

3. Thelma likes to _____ her bicycle.

   _____ her bicycle every day.

   _____ her bicycle yesterday.

   _____ her bicycle tomorrow.

4. My parents like to _____ .

   _____ every day.

   _____ yesterday.

   _____ tomorrow.

5. My wife and I like to _____ cookies.

   _____ cookies every day.

   _____ cookies yesterday.

   _____ cookies tomorrow.

6. Brian likes to _____ sailing.

   _____ sailing every day.

   _____ sailing yesterday.

   _____ sailing tomorrow.

| clean | cook | drive | eat | feed | go | read | take | wait | watch |

| like to | don't like to |
| likes to | doesn't like to |

1. Ronald _____likes to cook_____ spaghetti.

2. Sally _____doesn't like to take_____ the subway.

3. My children _____ the birds in the park.

4. Ted and Amy _____ in noisy restaurants.

5. My wife _____ novels.

6. Arnold _____ for the bus.

7. My friends and I _____ videos.

8. I _____ downtown.

9. Howard _____ his house.

10. Tim and Jim _____ to the doctor.

E WRITE ABOUT YOURSELF

What do you like to do?

I like to ....
I ....
I ....
I ....
I ....

What don't you like to do?

I don't like to ....
I ....
I ....
I ....
I ....

F DAY AFTER DAY

do	get up	go	make	plant	play	study	visit	wash	write

1. Tim _____washes_____ his car every day.

   _____He washed_____ his car yesterday.

   _____He's going to wash_____ his car tomorrow.

3. Millie and Max _____ dancing every Friday.

   _____ dancing last Friday.

   _____ dancing next Friday.

2. Alice _____ early every morning.

   _____ early yesterday morning.

   _____ early tomorrow morning.

4. I _____ English every evening.

   _____ English yesterday evening.

   _____ English tomorrow evening.

   (continued)

5. The man next door _____ the drums every night.

_____ the drums last night.

_____ the drums tomorrow night.

6. My mother _____ pancakes for breakfast every Sunday.

_____ pancakes last Sunday.

_____ pancakes next Sunday.

7. My wife and I _____ flowers every spring.

_____ flowers last spring.

_____ flowers next spring.

8. Steven _____ to his girlfriend every week.

_____ to her last week.

_____ to her next week.

9. Julie _____ her grandparents every weekend.

_____ them last weekend.

_____ them next weekend.

10. My husband and I _____ yoga every afternoon.

_____ yoga yesterday afternoon.

_____ yoga tomorrow afternoon.

11. I .... every ....

....

....

G GRAMMARRAP: *I Don't Like to Rush*

Listen. Then clap and practice.

I don't like to rush. Do you?
I don't like to hurry.
I don't like to get upset.
I don't like to worry.

I'm not going to rush. Are you?
I'm not going to hurry.
I'm not going to get upset.
I'm not going to worry!

H GRAMMARRAP: *He Doesn't Like to Watch TV*

Listen. Then clap and practice.

He doesn't like to watch TV.
He doesn't like to dance.
He doesn't like to cook or sew
or wash or iron his pants.

She doesn't like to go to the beach.
She doesn't like to shop.
She doesn't like to vacuum her rugs
or dust or wax or mop.

I WHAT'S PAULA GOING TO GIVE HER FAMILY?

cell phone
gloves
CD player
novel
dog
plant
watch
sweater

Paula is looking for presents for her family.
Here's what she's going to give them.

1. Her husband's hands are always cold. _____She's going to give him gloves._____

2. Her daughter loves animals. _____

3. Her son never arrives on time. _____

4. Her parents like to listen to music. _____

5. Her sister likes clothes. _____

6. Her brother likes to read. _____

7. Her grandparents like flowers. _____

8. Her cousin Charlie likes to talk to his friends. _____

J PRESENTS

1. Last year I ___gave___ my husband
   pajamas.

   This year _____I'm going to give him_____
   a bathrobe.

2. Last year Bobby _____ his grandmother
   candy.

   This year _____
   flowers.

3. Last year Carol _____ her boyfriend
   a tee shirt.

   This year _____
   sweat pants.

4. Last year we _____ our children
   a bird.

   This year _____
   a dog.

5. Last year I _____ my girlfriend
   perfume.

   This year _____
   a ring.

6. Last year we _____ our son
   a sweater.

   This year _____
   a bicycle.

7. Last year I ....

   This year ....

   ....

| he | her | him | I | me | she | they | them | us | we | you |

1. A. What did you give your wife for her birthday?

   B. _____I_____ gave ____her____ earrings.

2. A. What did your children give you for your birthday?

   B. _____ gave _____ a book.

3. A. What did Michael give his parents for their anniversary?

   B. _____ gave _____ a CD player.

4. A. What did your friends give you and your husband for your anniversary?

   B. _____ gave _____ a plant.

5. A. What did your wife give you for your birthday?

   B. _____ gave _____ a briefcase.

6. A. What did you and your wife give your son for his birthday?

   B. _____ gave _____ a bicycle.

7. A. I forget. What did you give me for my last birthday?

   B. _____ gave _____ a painting.

8. A. I forget. What did I give you for *your* last birthday?

   B. _____ gave _____ a dress.

1st	first	7th	seventh	13th	thirteenth	19th	nineteenth	50th	fiftieth
2nd	second	8th	eighth	14th	fourteenth	20th	twentieth	60th	sixtieth
3rd	third	9th	ninth	15th	fifteenth	21st	twenty-first	70th	seventieth
4th	fourth	10th	tenth	16th	sixteenth	22nd	twenty-second	80th	eightieth
5th	fifth	11th	eleventh	17th	seventeenth	30th	thirtieth	90th	ninetieth
6th	sixth	12th	twelfth	18th	eighteenth	40th	fortieth	100th	one hundredth

L MATCHING

__b__ 1. eighth   **a.** 2nd

_____ 2. one hundredth   **b.** 8th

_____ 3. second   **c.** 20th

_____ 4. twentieth   **d.** 100th

_____ 5. thirty-third   **e.** 14th

_____ 6. thirteenth   **f.** 13th

_____ 7. fourteenth   **g.** 40th

_____ 8. fortieth   **h.** 33rd

M WHAT'S THE NUMBER?

1. fiftieth   _____50th_____

2. ninety-ninth   _____

3. fifteenth   _____

4. twelfth   _____

5. seventy-seventh   _____

6. first   _____

7. sixteenth   _____

8. sixty-fifth   _____

9. eighty-fourth   _____

10. thirty-sixth   _____

N LISTENING

Listen and write the ordinal number you hear.

1. barber shop   _____2nd_____

2. Wong family   _____

3. Acme Company   _____

4. Bob Richards   _____

5. bank   _____

6. dentist's office   _____

7. flower shop   _____

8. Martinez family   _____

9. Louise Lane   _____

10. computer store   _____

11. French restaurant   _____

12. my apartment   _____

13. Park family   _____

14. Dr. Jacobson   _____

15. Walker family   _____

16. health club   _____

O RICHARD'S BIRTHDAYS

Fill in the missing words.

On Richard's 7th birthday, he (have) ___had___¹ a party at home. His mother (make) _____² pizza, and his father (bake) _____³ a cake. Richard's parents (give) _____⁴ him a new dog. Richard's friends (love) _____⁵ his birthday party because they (play) _____⁶ with his new dog, but Richard was upset because his mother didn't (give) _____⁷ the dog any cake to eat.

On Richard's 10th birthday, he (go) _____⁸ to the beach with his friends. They (swim) _____⁹ at the beach, and they (go) _____¹⁰ to a restaurant to eat. Richard's friends (like) _____¹¹ his birthday party, but Richard was upset because he didn't (like) _____¹² his present. His friends (give) _____¹³ him a wallet, but he (want) _____¹⁴ a baseball.

On Richard's 13th birthday, he (have) _____¹⁵ a picnic. His mother (cook) _____¹⁶ hot dogs and hamburgers. They (eat) _____¹⁷ delicious food and (play) _____¹⁸ baseball. All of his friends (enjoy) _____¹⁹ his birthday party, but Richard was upset because the girls didn't (talk) _____²⁰ to him.

On Richard's 16th birthday, he didn't (have) _____²¹ a party. He (go) _____²² dancing with his girlfriend, and he (have) _____²³ a wonderful time. His friends didn't (give) _____²⁴ him presents and his parents didn't (cook) _____²⁵. But Richard wasn't upset because he (dance) _____²⁶ with his girlfriend all night.

P MATCHING

_b_ 1. Richard didn't like his present _____.

____ 2. He went dancing _____.

____ 3. His parents gave him a dog _____.

____ 4. The girls didn't talk to Richard _____.

a. on his 7th birthday

b. on his 10th birthday

c. on his 13th birthday

d. on his 16th birthday

apples	cheese	ice cream	meat	pepper
bread	eggs	ketchup	mustard	potatoes
cake	flour	lettuce	onions	soy sauce
carrots	grapes	mayonnaise	oranges	tomatoes

1. _____tomatoes_____   2. _____carrots_____   3. _____grapes_____   4. _____potatoes_____

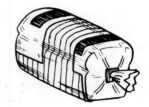

5. _____icecream_____   6. _____apples_____   7. _____lettuce_____   8. _____bread_____

9. _____cake_____   10. _____flour_____   11. _____onions_____   12. _____ketchup_____

13. _____mayonnaise_____ 14. _____eggs_____   15. _____meat_____   16. _____oranges_____

17. _____mustard_____   18. _____pepper_____   19. _____cheese_____   20. _____

WHAT ARE THEY SAYING?

| Where's | Where are | It's | They're |

1. A. _____Where's_____ the butter?

   B. _____It's_____ in the refrigerator.

2. A. _____Where are_____ the bananas?

   B. _____They're_____ on the counter.

3. A. _____where's_____ the salt?

   B. _____It's_____ in the cabinet.

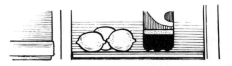

4. A. _____where are_____ the lemons?

   B. _____They're_____ in the refrigerator.

5. A. _____where's_____ the cookies?

   B. _____It's_____ in the cabinet.

6. A. _____where are_____ the chicken?

   B. _____They're_____ in the freezer.

7. A. _____where are_____ the pears?

   B. _____They're_____ on the counter.

8. A. _____where's_____ the rice?

   B. _____It's_____ in the cabinet.

C **LISTENING**

Listen and choose the correct response.

1. (a.) It's on the counter.
   b. They're on the counter.

2. a. It's in the refrigerator.
   b. They're in the refrigerator.

3. a. It's in the freezer.
   b. They're in the freezer.

4. a. It's in the cabinet.
   b. They're in the cabinet.

5. a. It's on the counter.
   b. They're on the counter.

6. a. It's in the cabinet.
   b. They're in the cabinet.

7. a. It's on the counter.
   b. They're on the counter.

8. a. It's in the refrigerator.
   b. They're in the refrigerator.

Look at the menu to see what Randy's Restaurant has and doesn't have today.

Today's Menu
spaghetti
hamburgers
salad
ice cream
apple pie
milk
soda

1. A. May I have a hamburger and some french fries?

    B. I'm sorry, but _____ there aren't _____

    _____ any french fries _____ .

2. A. May I please have a salad and some tea?

    B. I'm sorry, but _____ there isn't _____

    _____ any tea _____ .

3. A. May I have chicken and some milk?

    B. I'm sorry, but _____ there isn't _____

    _____ any chicken _____ .

4. A. May I have ice cream and some cookies?

    B. I'm sorry, but _____ there aren't _____

    _____ any cookies _____ .

5. A. May I have cake and some soda?

    B. I'm sorry, but _____ there isn't _____

    _____ any cake _____ .

6. A. May we have two sandwiches, please?

    B. I'm sorry, but _____ there aren't _____

    _____ any sandwiches _____

7. A. May I have apple pie and some orange juice?

    B. I'm sorry, but _____ there isn't _____

    _____ any orange juice _____ .

8. A. May I have spaghetti and some meatballs?

    B. I'm sorry, but _____ there aren't _____

    _____ any meatballs _____ .

E THERE ISN'T/THERE AREN'T

1. There _____isn't any mayonnaise_____.

   How about some _____mustard_____?

2. There _____aren't any bananas_____.

   How about some _____grapes_____?

3. There _____aren't any meat_____.

   How about some _____fish_____?

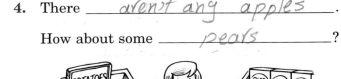

4. There _____aren't any apples_____.

   How about some _____pears_____?

5. There _____isn't any icecream_____

   How about some _____yogurt_____?

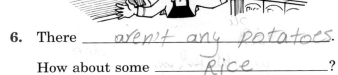

6. There _____aren't any potatoes.

   How about some _____Rice_____?

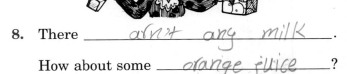

7. There _____aren't any tomatoes.

   How about some _____onions_____?

8. There _____aren't any milk_____.

   How about some _____orange juice_____?

F LISTENING

Listen and put a check (✓) under the correct picture.

1. _____   ✔

2. _____   _____

3. _____   _____

4. _____

5. _____   _____

6. _____   _____

morina

G WHAT'S THE WORD?

| how much | too much | how many | too many | a little | a few |

1. A. _____How many_____ meatballs do you want?

   B. Not _____too many_____.

   Just _____a few_____.

2. A. _____How much_____ cheese do you want?

   B. Not _____too much_____.

   Just _____a little_____.

3. A. _____How much_____ ice cream do you want?

   B. Not _____too much_____.

   Just _____a little_____.

4. A. _____How many_____ cookies do you want?

   B. Not _____too many_____.

   Just _____a few_____.

5. A. _____How much_____ lemonade do you want?

   B. Not _____too much_____.

   Just _____a little_____.

6. A. _____How many_____ oranges do you want?

   B. Not _____too many_____.

   Just _____a few_____.

H WHAT'S THE PROBLEM?

| too much | too many |

1. She cooked _____too many_____ meatballs.

2. He drinks _____too much_____ soda.

3. They ate _____too much_____ ice cream.

4. Henry had _____too many_____ onions.

Listen. Then clap and practice.

A. How much salt should I put in the soup?

B. Just a little, not too much.

A. How many onions should I put in the salad?

B. Just a few, not too many.

A. How much pepper should I put in the stew?

B. Just a little, not too much.

A. How many eggs should I put in the omelet?

B. Just a few, not too many.

A. How much sugar should I put in the tea?

B. Just a little, not too much.

All. Salt in the soup,

Pepper in the stew,

Eggs in the omelet,

Just a few.

Just a little, not too much.

Not too many, just a few.

Just a few, not too many.

Not too many, just one or two.

Activity Workbook 17

| little | much | this | | is | it's | | it |
| few | many | | these | are | they're | | them |

1. A. Would you care for some more chocolate cake?

    B. Yes, please. But only a ___little___.

        My dentist says I eat too ___much___ chocolate cake.

2. A. Would you care for some more french fries?

    B. Yes, please. But only a _a few_.

        My wife says I eat too _many_ french fries.

3. A. _would you_ pizza _some more_ fantastic.

    B. I'm glad you like _____. Would you care for a _____ more?

    A. Yes, please.

4. A. _____ potatoes _____ good.

    B. I'm glad you like _____. Would you care for a _____ more?

    A. No, thank you.

5. A. Would you like a _____ yogurt?

    B. Yes, please. My doctor says _____ good for my health.

6. A. Would you care for some cookies? I baked _____ this morning.

    B. Yes, please. But just a _____.

7. A. Would you care for some more pie?

    B. Yes, please. I know _____ bad for my health, but I really like _____.

8. A. You're eating too _____ meatballs!

    B. I know. But _____ really good. Can I have just a _____ more?

K MATCHING

_e_   1. This pie is very good!

___   2. How do you like the hamburgers?

___   3. I think these cookies are excellent!

_c_   4. How much rice do you want?

_i_   5. Where's the tea?

___   6. Let's make some lemonade!

___   7. How do you like the pizza?

___   8. Where are the bananas?

___   9. How many carrots do you want?

___   10. Let's bake a cake for dessert!

a. We can't. There isn't any flour.

b. I think it's delicious.

c. Just a little.

d. They're on the counter.

e. I'm glad you like it.

f. Just a few.

g. We can't. There aren't any lemons.

h. I'm glad you like them.

i. It's in the cabinet.

j. I think they're delicious.

L LISTENING

Listen and put a check (✓) under the correct picture.

1. ___   ✓

2.  ___   ___

3.  ___   ___

4. ___    ___

5. ___   ___

6.  ___   ___

7.  ___   ___

8. ___   ___

9.  ___    ___

10. ___   ___

Listen. Then clap and practice.

All.	Not too	much, just	a little,
	Not too	many, just	a few.
	Not too	much, just	a little,
	Not too	many, just	a few.

A.	Would you	like more	chicken?
B.	Just	a little.	
A.	Would you	like more	carrots?
B.	Just	a few.	
A.	Would you	like more	gravy?
B.	Just	a little.	
A.	Would you	like more	mushrooms?
B.	Just	a few.	
A.	Would you	like more	salad?
B.	Just	a little.	
A.	Would you	like more	tomatoes?
B.	Just	a few.	
A.	Would you	like more	coffee?
B.	Just	a little.	
A.	Would you	like more	cookies?
B.	Just	a few.	

All.	Not too	much, just	a little.
	Not too	many, just	a few.
	Not too	much, just	a little.
	Not too	many, just	a few.

3

bag	bunch	~~can~~	gallon	jar	loaf/loaves
bottle	~~box~~	~~dozen~~	head	pound	~~of~~

1. Jack is going to buy food at the supermarket.

Jack's Shopping List

a _____can_____ _of_ soup

a _____head_____ _of_ lettuce

a _____bottle_____ _of_ ketchup

a _____pound_____ _of_ cheese

a _____bag_____ _of_ flour

2. Jennifer is going to make breakfast for her parents.

Jennifer's Shopping List

a _____box_____ _of_ cereal

a _____jar_____ _of_ jam

a _____loaf_____ _of_ bread

a _____bunch_____ _of_ bananas

a _____a dozen_____ eggs

3. Mr. and Mrs. Baxter are going to have a birthday party for their daughter.

The Baxters' Shopping List

3 _____gallon_____ _of_ ice cream

2 _____boxs_____ _of_ cookies

2 _____bags_____ _of_ grapes

3 _____pounds_____ _of_ meat

2 _____loaves_____ _of_ bread

4. What are YOU going to buy this week?

Your Shopping List

....

....

....

....

....

B WHAT ARE THEY SAYING?

bananas	cheese	cookies	ice cream	jam	onions

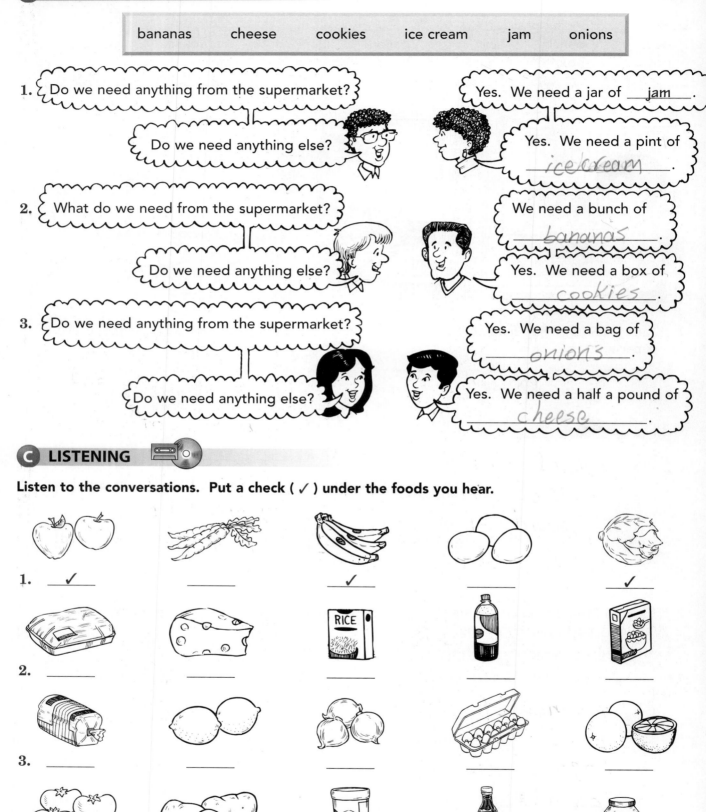

1. Do we need anything from the supermarket?

Do we need anything else?

Yes. We need a jar of ___jam___.

Yes. We need a pint of __ice cream__.

2. What do we need from the supermarket?

Do we need anything else?

We need a bunch of __bananas__.

Yes. We need a box of __cookies__.

3. Do we need anything from the supermarket?

Do we need anything else?

Yes. We need a bag of __onions__.

Yes. We need a half a pound of __cheese__.

C LISTENING

Listen to the conversations. Put a check (✓) under the foods you hear.

1.   ✓   ✓   ✓

2.

3.

4.

GRAMMARRAP: *We Need Food*

Listen. Then clap and practice.

All. We need bread.

Whole wheat bread.

A. How many loaves do we need?

All. Two.

All. We need beans.

Black beans.

B. How many cans do we need?

All. Three.

All. We need rice.

Brown rice.

C. How many pounds do we need?

All. Four.

All. We need jam.

Strawberry jam.

D. How many jars do we need?

All. Five.

All. We need milk.

Fresh milk.

E. How many quarts do we need?

All. Six.

All. We need cash.

We need money.

F. How much money do we need?

All. A lot!

are	cost	does	loaf	money	of	quart
bread	costs	is	loaves	much	pound	right

1. A. How __much__ does a _____ of milk _____?

   B. A _____ of _____ _____ two thirty-nine.

   A. Two dollars and thirty-nine cents?! That's a lot of _____!

   B. You're _____. Milk _____ very expensive this week.

2. A. How _____ does a _____ _____ bread cost?

   B. A _____ of _____ _____ one twenty-nine.

   A. Good! I'll take six _____, please.

   B. Six _____?! That's a lot _____ bread!

   A. I know. But _____ _____ very cheap this week!

3. A. How _____ _____ a _____ of apples cost?

   B. A _____ _____ apples _____ three sixty-five.

   A. Three sixty five?! That's too _____ money!

   B. You're right. Apples _____ very expensive today,

   but bananas _____ very cheap.

   A. That's nice. But how can I make an apple pie with bananas?!

F **LISTENING**

Listen and circle the price you hear.

1. $1.95   ($1.99)   4. $25   25¢   7. $3.13 $3.30

2. $5   5¢   5. $2.74 $2.47   8. $1.15 $1.50

3. $4.79 $9.47   6. $6.60 $6.16   9. $2.10 $21

1. A. What would you like for breakfast?
    B. Please give me an order of _____.
        a. cereal
        (b.) scrambled eggs

2. A. What would you like to drink?
    B. I want a glass of _____.
        a. milk
        b. coffee

3. A. What would you like for lunch?
    B. I want a bowl of _____.
        a. pancakes
        b. soup

4. A. Would you care for some dessert?
    B. Yes. I'd like a dish of _____.
        a. ice cream
        b. hot chocolate

5. A. What would you like?
    B. Please give me a cup of _____.
        a. tea
        b. cake

6. A. What would you like for dessert?
    B. I'd like a piece of _____.
        a. strawberries
        b. apple pie

H **WHERE WOULD YOU LIKE TO GO FOR LUNCH?**

are	glass	many	order
bowl	is	much	piece
cup	it	of	they
dish			

A. Where would you like to go for lunch?

B. Let's go to Carla's Cafe. Their spaghetti ___is___¹ out of this world and _____² isn't expensive. I had an _____³ _____⁴ spaghetti there last week for a dollar ninety-five.

A. I don't really want to go to Carla's Cafe. Their spaghetti _____⁵ very good, but you can't get any chocolate milk. I like to have a _____⁶ of chocolate milk with my lunch.

B. How about The Pancake Place? Their pancakes _____⁷ fantastic, and _____⁸ aren't expensive. An _____⁹ _____¹⁰ pancakes costs two sixty-nine.

A. I really don't like The Pancake Place. The pancakes _____¹¹ tasty, but their salad _____¹² terrible! It has too _____¹³ lettuce and too _____¹⁴ onions.

B. Well, how about Rita's Restaurant? Their desserts are wonderful. You can get a delicious _____¹⁵ _____¹⁶ pie, a _____¹⁷ _____¹⁸ strawberries, or a _____¹⁹ _____²⁰ ice cream.

A. I know. But their hot chocolate _____²¹ very bad. I like to have a _____²² _____²³ hot chocolate with my dessert.

B. Wait a minute! I know where we can go for lunch. Let's go to YOUR house!

I GRAMMARRAP: *Grocery List*

Listen. Then clap and practice.

We need a loaf of   bread

And a jar of   jam,

A box of   cookies

And a pound of   ham.

A bottle of   ketchup,

A pound of   cheese,

A dozen   eggs,

And a can of   peas.

A head of   lettuce,

Half a pound of   rice,

A bunch of   bananas,

And a bag of   ice.

a loaf of bread
a jar of jam
a box of cookies
a pound of ham
a bottle of ketchup

J GRAMMARRAP: *What Would You Like to Have?*

Listen. Then clap and practice.

A. What would you like to   order?

What would you like to   have?

B. An order of   chicken,   a dish of   potatoes,

A large green   salad   with a lot of   tomatoes.

A bowl of   soup,   an order of   rice,

And a glass of   soda   with a lot of   ice.

A. And what would you like for   dessert?

B. Nothing,   thanks.   I'm not very   hungry!

WHAT'S THE WORD?

1. Slice the | honey / (carrots) | .

5. Slice the | baking soda / apples | .

2. Cut up the | oranges / salt | .

6. Pour it into the mixing | bowl / recipe | .

3. Chop up the | flour / nuts | .

7. Mix in / Put | the raisins.

4. Pour in the | water / potatoes | .

8. Add / Cook | for two hours.

L **WHAT'S THE RECIPE?**

| a little   a few |

Millie's Tomato Sauce

1. Put ____a little____ butter into a pan.

2. Chop up _____ onions.

3. Cut up _____ mushrooms and _____ cheese.

4. Slice _____ tomatoes.

5. Add _____ salt and _____ pepper.

6. Cook for _____ minutes.

M **LISTENING**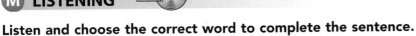

Listen and choose the correct word to complete the sentence.

1. a. onions
   (b.) water

2. a. cheese
   b. nuts

3. a. oranges
   b. baking soda

4. a. salt
   b. raisins

5. a. tomato
   b. potatoes

6. a. pepper
   b. mushrooms

Activity Workbook   **27**

A. Fill in the blanks.

Ex. a _____quart_____
of milk

1. a _____
of bananas

2. a _____
of soup

3. a _____
of onions

4. a _____
of pie

5. 2 _____
of cereal

6. 2 _____
of bread

B. Circle the correct answers.

Ex. Yogurt (is)
         are   cheap today.

1. I eat too much
                many   cookies.

2. She ate so much
                 many   cake that

she has a stomachache.

3. What do you like
                  like to   do on the

weekend?

4. How much
          many   does a bowl of

strawberries cost?

5. Would you care for a little
                          few   grapes?

I bought it
           them   this morning, and

it's
they're   very fresh.

6. This   rice is
    These   are   delicious. May I

have a little
         few   more?

C. Complete the sentences.

Ex. Janet watches TV every Friday.

  She watched TV last Friday.

  She's going to watch TV next Friday.

1. Alan drives to the mall every week.

He _____ to the mall last week.

_____

to the mall next week.

2. I go on vacation every year.

I _____ on vacation last year.

_____

on vacation next year.

3. We play baseball every Saturday.

We _____ baseball last Saturday.

_____ baseball next Saturday.

4. My sister writes letters to her friends every weekend.

She _____ letters to her friends last weekend.

_____ letters to her friends next weekend.

5. Ed makes pancakes every morning.

He _____ pancakes yesterday morning.

_____ pancakes tomorrow morning.

D. Complete the sentences.

Ex. Last year my parents gave me a sweater for my birthday.

This year _____*they're going to give me*_____ a jacket.

1. Last year Tom gave his girlfriend flowers.

This year _____

_____ candy.

2. Last year Sue gave her husband a CD player.

This year _____

_____ a briefcase.

3. Last year we gave our parents a cell phone.

This year _____

_____ a computer.

E. Listen and circle the correct word.

"I'm sorry, but there _____ any."

Ex. isn't
(aren't)

3. isn't
aren't

1. isn't
aren't

4. isn't
aren't

2. isn't
aren't

5. isn't
aren't

1. A. Will you be back soon?

B. Yes, _____I will_____. _____I'll_____

_____be back_____ in half an hour.

2. A. Will the game begin soon?

B. Yes, _____. _____

_____ in ten minutes.

3. A. Will Henry return soon?

B. Yes, _____. _____

_____ in a week.

4. A. Will we be ready soon?

B. Yes, _____. _____

_____ in a little while.

5. A. Will Grandma and Grandpa arrive soon?

B. Yes, _____. _____

_____ in 15 or 20 minutes.

6. A. Will the storm end soon?

B. Yes, _____. _____

_____ in a few hours.

7. A. Will Kate be here soon?

B. Yes, _____. _____

_____ in a few minutes.

8. A. Will you get out soon?

B. Yes, _____. _____

_____ in a month.

B WE'LL JUST HAVE TO WAIT AND SEE

1. Do you think Barbara ___will___ move to a new apartment soon?

   I don't know. Maybe ___she___ ___will___, and maybe ___she___ ___won't___.

2. Do you think Robert _____ like his new job?

   I don't know. Maybe _____, and maybe _____.

3. Do you think _____ drive to the beach this weekend?

   I don't know. Maybe I _____, and maybe _____.

4. Do you think _____ be a famous scientist some day?

   I don't know. Maybe you _____, and maybe _____.

5. Do you think _____ snow a lot this winter?

   I don't know. Maybe _____, and maybe _____.

6. Do you think _____ _____ be a lot of traffic today?

   I don't know. Maybe _____, and maybe _____.

7. Do you think you and Roger _____ get married soon?

   I don't know. Maybe _____, and maybe _____.

8. Do you think the guests _____ like the fruitcake?

   I don't know. Maybe _____, and maybe _____.

C WHAT DO YOU THINK?

		Yes!	No!
1.	What will Charlie bake for the party?	Maybe _____he'll_____ _____bake_____ cookies.	I'm sure _____he_____ _____won't bake_____ a cake.
2.	What will Mom order at the restaurant?	Maybe _____ _____ a sandwich.	I'm sure _____ _____ a pizza.
3.	Where will your parents go this evening?	Maybe _____ _____ to a movie.	I'm sure _____ _____ to a party.
4.	What will you get for your birthday?	Maybe _____ _____ a sweater.	I'm sure _____ _____ a cell phone.
5.	When will the train arrive?	Maybe _____ _____ in an hour.	I'm sure _____ _____ on time.
6.	When will we finish our English book?	Maybe _____ _____ it in a few months.	I'm sure _____ _____ it next week.

D LISTENING

Listen and circle the words you hear.

1. won't / (want to)

2. won't / want to

3. won't / want to

4. won't / want to

5. won't / want to

6. won't / want to

7. won't / want to

8. won't / want to

E DIFFERENT OPINIONS

1. I think the weather will be nice tomorrow. Everybody else thinks ____it 'll be____ bad.

2. My wife thinks the guests will arrive on time. I think _____ late.

3. I think our daughter will be a lawyer. My husband thinks _____ an architect.

4. My parents think my brother Bob will buy a bicycle. I think _____ a motorcycle.

5. I think we'll have a good time at the party. My husband thinks _____ a terrible time.

I'm afraid → I think

Listen. Then clap and practice.

A.   I'll   remember.

B.   Are you   sure?

A.   Don't   worry.   I'll remember.   You'll see.

A.   He'll   do it.

B.   Are you   sure?

A.   Don't   worry.   He'll do it.   You'll see.

A.   She'll   call you.

B.   Are you   sure?

A.   Don't   worry.   She'll call you.   You'll see.

A.   It'll be   ready.

B.   Are you   sure?

A.   Don't   worry.   It'll be ready.   You'll see.

A.   We'll   be there.

B.   Are you   sure?

A.   Don't   worry.   We'll be there.   You'll see.

A.   They'll   get there.

B.   Are you   sure?

A.   Don't   worry.   They'll get there.   You'll see.

1. A. What's Bruno going to make for breakfast this morning?

   B. _____He might make eggs_____, or

   _____he might make pancakes_____.

2. A. What time is Sally going to get up tomorrow morning on her day off?

   B. _____, or

   _____.

3. A. When are your children going to clean their bedroom?

   B. _____, or

   _____.

4. A. What are you going to give your parents for their anniversary?

   B. _____, or

   _____.

5. A. What are you and your friends going to watch on TV tonight?

   B. _____, or

   _____.

6. A. Where are Mr. and Mrs. Martinez going to go for their vacation?

   B. _____, or

   _____.

7. A. Tell me, what are you going to do this weekend?

   B. _____, or

   _____.

8. A. What's Arthur going to name his new cat?

   B. _____, or

   _____.

BE CAREFUL!

1. Don't stand there!
   (a.) You might get hit.
   b. You might watch.

2. Put on your safety glasses!
   a. You might hurt your ears.
   b. You might hurt your eyes.

3. Don't touch those wires!
   a. You might get a shock.
   b. You might get cold.

4. Don't touch that machine!
   a. You might get hurt.
   b. You might get a helmet.

5. Watch your step!
   a. You might finish.
   b. You might fall.

6. Put on your helmet!
   a. You might hurt your back.
   b. You might hurt your head.

I **LOUD AND CLEAR** W!

winter	Wendy	walk	weather	work

1. ___Wendy___ doesn't like to ___walk___ to ___work___ in the ___winter___ when the ___weather___ is bad.

wet	walk	waiter	won't	waitress

2. The _____ and the _____ _____ _____ there. The floor is _____!

wife	wash	Walter	windows	want	weekend

3. _____ and his _____ _____ to _____ their _____ this _____.

wasn't	we	water	wanted	warm

4. _____ _____ _____ to go swimming, but the _____ _____ _____.

break her leg	fall asleep	get fat	have a terrible time	rain
catch a cold	get a backache	get seasick	look terrible	step on her feet
drown	get a sunburn	get sick	miss our bus	

1. Jennifer won't go skating because

___she's afraid she might___

___break her leg___ .

2. George won't go to the beach because

_____

_____ .

3. I won't go swimming because

_____

_____ .

4. We won't have lunch with you because

_____

_____ .

5. My mother and father won't go on the roller

coaster because _____

_____ .

6. Brian won't go dancing with Brenda

because _____

_____ .

7. We won't go to a play because

_____

_____ .

8. I won't go to Patty's party because

_____

_____ .

9. Barry won't carry those boxes because

_____

_____ .

10. Sally won't go sailing because

_____

_____ .

11. I won't eat dessert because

_____

_____ .

12. Helen won't take a walk in the park because

_____

_____ .

13. We won't wash our clothes today because

_____

_____ .

14. Fred won't get a short haircut because

_____

_____ .

K LISTENING

Listen and choose the correct answer.

1. a. He doesn't want to go on the roller coaster.
   b. He doesn't want to go to the doctor.

2. a. She doesn't want to go skiing.
   b. She doesn't want to go to the movies.

3. a. He doesn't want to go to a play.
   b. He doesn't want to go dancing.

4. a. She doesn't want to go skiing.
   b. She doesn't want to stay home.

5. a. He doesn't want to read a book.
   b. He doesn't want to take a walk in the park.

6. a. He doesn't want to go swimming.
   b. He doesn't want to go dancing.

7. a. She doesn't want to go skating.
   b. She doesn't want to go sailing.

8. a. He doesn't want to go to the library.
   b. He doesn't want to go to the beach.

9. a. She doesn't want to go to the party.
   b. She doesn't want to eat dinner.

10. a. He doesn't want to get a short haircut.
    b. He doesn't want to buy a small dog.

Listen. Then clap and practice.

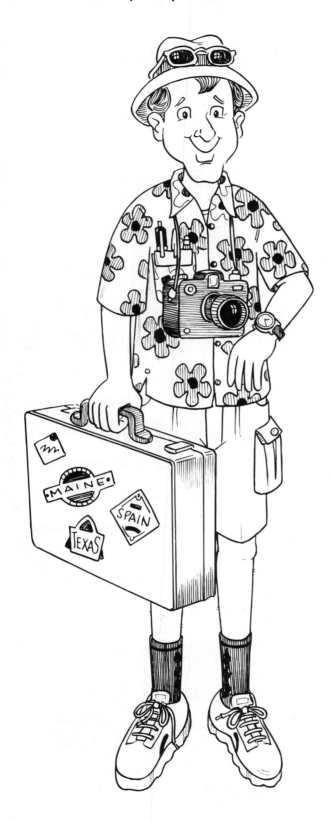

A.   When is he going to   leave?

B.   He might leave at   noon.

C.   He might leave on   Monday.

D.   He might leave in   June.

A.   Where is he going to   go?

B.   He might go to   Spain.

C.   He might go to   Texas.

D.   He might go to   Maine.

A.   How is he going to   get there?

B.   He might go by   train.

C.   He might take the   bus.

D.   He might take a   plane.

A.   Who is he going to   go with?

B.   He might go with   Ed.

C.   He might go with   Peter.

D.   He might go with   Fred.

A.   What's he going to   do there?

B.   He might see the   zoo.

C.   He might take some   pictures.

D.   He might write to   you.

M GRAMMARSONG: *We Really Can't Decide*

Listen and fill in the words to the song. Then listen again and sing along.

cake	decide	go	her	make	Mexico	sweater	wide

I want to cook some dinner.

I don't know what to ___make___ 1.

I might make stew. I might make eggs.

I might just bake a _____ 2.

I really don't know what to cook.

The choices are so _____ 3.

I might cook this. I might cook that.

I really can't _____ 4.

I'm planning my vacation.

I don't know where to _____ 5.

I might see France. I might see Spain.

I might see _____ 6.

I really don't know where to go.

The choices are so _____ 7.

I might go here. I might go there.

I really can't _____ 8.

I'm buying Mom a present.

I don't know what to get _____ 9.

I might buy gloves. I might buy boots.

I might get her a _____ 10.

I really don't know what to get.

The choices are so _____ 11.

I might get this. I might get that.

I really can't _____ 12.

Activity Workbook   **39**

1. Henry's old sofa was soft. His new sofa is _____ *softer* _____.

2. Nancy's old briefcase was light. Her new briefcase is _____.

3. Bob's old living room was large. His new living room is _____.

4. My old recipe for chili was hot. My new recipe is _____.

5. My old boss was friendly. My new boss is _____.

6. Our old neighborhood was safe. Our new neighborhood is _____.

7. Linda's old cell phone was small. Her new cell phone is _____.

8. Grandpa's old sports car was fancy. His new sports car is _____.

9. Cathy's old mittens were warm. Her new mittens are _____.

10. Billy's old school was big. His new school is _____.

11. My old job was easy. My new job is _____.

12. Our old neighbors were nice. Our new neighbors are _____.

13. Richard's old watch was cheap. His new watch is _____.

14. Dr. Green's old office was ugly. His new office is _____.

B WHAT'S THE WORD?

 Tim Jim

1. A. Is Tim's hair short?

   B. Yes, but Jim's hair is _____ *shorter* _____.

2. A. Is Charlie's cat cute?

   B. Yes, but his dog is _____.

 Barbara  Betty

3. A. Is Debbie's dog fat?

   B. Yes, but her cat is _____.

4. A. Is Barbara busy?

   B. Yes, but Betty is _____.

C THEY'RE DIFFERENT

1. Paul's parrot is talkative, but Paula's parrot is _____more talkative_____.
2. Your roommate is interesting, but my roommate is _____.
3. Sam's suit is attractive, but Stanley's suit is _____.
4. Shirley's shoes are comfortable, but her sister's shoes are _____.
5. George is intelligent, but his brother is _____.
6. My daughter's hair is long, but my son's hair is _____.
7. Last winter was cold, but this winter is _____.
8. William is thin, but his father is _____.
9. My children are healthy, but my doctor's children are _____.
10. John's computer is powerful, but Jane's computer is _____.
11. Barbara's boyfriend is handsome, but her father is _____.
12. My teeth are white, but my dentist's teeth are _____.
13. Our neighbor's yard is beautiful, but our yard is _____.

D WHAT'S THE WORD?

1. A. This meatloaf is delicious.
   B. It's very good, but my mother's meatloaf is _____more delicious_____.

2. A. Chicken is good for you.
   B. I know. But everybody says that fish is _____ for you.

3. A. This necklace is very expensive.
   B. You're right. But that necklace is _____.

4. A. You're very energetic!
   B. Yes, I am. But my wife is _____.

Activity Workbook **41**

Across

4. My upstairs neighbor is friendly, but my downstairs neighbor is _____.
7. Their baby is cute, but my baby is _____.
8. Betty's blue dress is pretty, but her green dress is _____.
11. This bicycle is fast, but that bicycle is _____.
12. My old apartment was large, but my new apartment is _____.
13. Your dishwasher is quiet, but my dishwasher is _____.

Down

1. Our old rug was soft, but our new rug is _____.
2. Yesterday it was warm, but today it's _____.
3. Their new house is small, but their old house was _____.
4. Tom's new tie is fancy, but his son's tie is _____.
5. My old tennis racket was light, but my new tennis racket is _____.
6. Bananas were cheap last week, but this week they're _____.
9. The chili we ate last week was hot, but this chili is _____.
10. This picture is ugly, but that picture is _____.

F LISTENING

Listen and choose the correct words to complete the sentences.

1. a. cooler
   b. cuter

2. a. smaller
   b. taller

3. a. more handsome
   b. more attractive

4. a. nicer
   b. lighter

5. a. fatter
   b. faster

6. a. friendlier
   b. fancier

7. a. more interesting
   b. more intelligent

8. a. bigger
   b. busier

cheap	delicious	fancy	small	talented	talkative

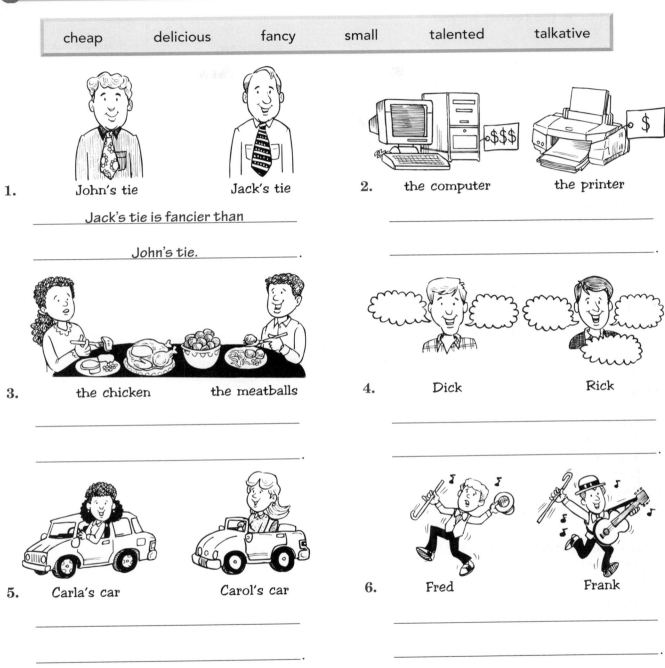

1. John's tie   Jack's tie

_____ Jack's tie is fancier than _____

_____ John's tie. _____.

2. the computer   the printer

_____

_____.

3. the chicken   the meatballs

_____

_____.

4. Dick   Rick

_____

_____.

5. Carla's car   Carol's car

_____

_____.

6. Fred   Frank

_____

_____.

H **GRAMMARRAP:** *Honey Is Sweeter Than Sugar*

Listen. Then clap and practice.

Honey is   sweeter than   sugar.

Coffee is   stronger than   tea.

Hours are   longer than   minutes.

Thirty is   larger than three.

Peaches are   softer than   apples.

Pepper is   hotter than   rice.

Pears are   bigger than   lemons.

Nothing is   colder than   ice.

LISTENING

Listen and circle the correct answer.

1. yesterday   Yes No   today

2. $2.50   Yes No $3.25

3. Betty   Yes No   Jane

4. Bob   Yes No   Bill

5. Barry   Yes No   Larry

6. science test   Yes No   history test

7. Irene   Yes No   Eileen

8. Ronald   Yes No   Donald

J **GRAMMARRAP:** *I Can't Decide*

Listen. Then clap and practice.

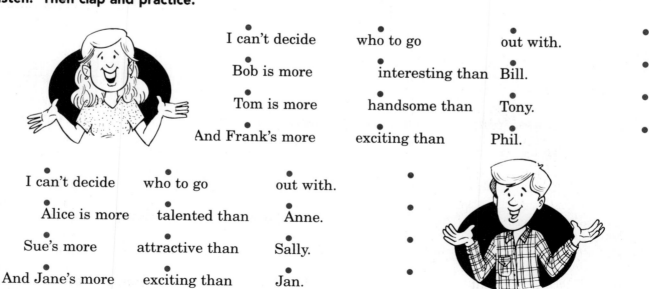

I can't decide   who to go   out with.
Bob is more   interesting than   Bill.
Tom is more   handsome than   Tony.
And Frank's more   exciting than   Phil.

I can't decide   who to go   out with.
Alice is more   talented than   Anne.
Sue's more   attractive than   Sally.
And Jane's more   exciting than   Jan.

K WHAT SHOULD THEY DO?

call the dentist	fire him	rent a video
call the police	hire her	plant some flowers

1. My garden looks terrible!

You should plant some flowers.

2. Harvey has a very bad toothache!

_____

3. My husband and I want to see a movie tonight.

4. A thief stole my daughter's new bicycle!

_____

5. The people at the Ace company think that Jennifer is capable and talented.

6. Ms. Hunter is upset because her secretary falls asleep at work every day.

_____

L GrammarRap: *Should They . . . ?*

Listen. Then clap and practice.

A. Should he   call or should he   write?

B. He should   call   tomorrow   night.

A. Should I   keep it or give it   back?

B. You should wear it or give it to   Jack.

A. Should I   stay or   should I   go?

B. Don't ask me.   I don't know.

Activity Workbook   **45**

1. Should I buy a van or a sports car?

   I think _____ you should buy a van _____
   because _____ vans are more useful than _____   *(or)*
   _____ sports cars _____ .

   I think _____ you should buy a sports car _____
   because _____ sports cars are more _____
   _____ exciting than vans _____ .

2. Should she buy a bicycle or a motorcycle?

   I think _____
   because _____
   _____ .

3. Should we move to Weston or Easton?

   I think _____
   because _____
   _____ .

4. Should he buy the fur hat or the leather hat?

   I think _____
   because _____
   _____ .

5. Should I vote for Alan Lane or George Gray?

   I think _____
   because _____
   _____ .

6. Should we hire Mr. Hall or Mr. Hill?

   I think _____
   because _____
   _____ .

7. Should he go out with Patty or Pam?

   I think _____
   because _____
   _____ .

N WHAT'S THE WORD?

mine	his	hers	ours	yours	theirs

1. A. Is this Michael's cell phone?

   B. No. It isn't _____ his _____ .

2. A. Are these your safety glasses?

   B. No. They aren't _____ .

3. A. Is this your sister's violin?

   B. No. It isn't _____ .

4. A. Is that Mr. and Mrs. Garcia's van?

   B. No. It isn't _____ .

5. A. Is this my recipe for fruitcake?

   B. No. It isn't _____ .

6. A. Are these your son's sneakers?

   B. No. They aren't _____ .

7. Is that your car?

   No. It isn't _____ .

O WHAT'S THE WORD?

1. You know, my parents aren't as sympathetic as your parents.

   Really? I think ((yours) your) are much more sympathetic than (my   mine).

2. Robert's cookies aren't as delicious as his sister's cookies.

   Really? I think (him   his) are much more delicious than (her   hers).

3. Our computer isn't as fast as their computer.

   Really? I think (ours   their) is much faster than (theirs   them).

4. My pronunciation isn't as good as your pronunciation.

   Don't be ridiculous! (Your   Yours) is much better than (mine   my).

5. Jane's briefcase isn't as attractive as her husband's briefcase.

   Really? I think (her   hers) is much more attractive than (him   his).

P DIFFERENT, BUT OKAY

1. My neighborhood (quiet) _____isn't as quiet as_____ your neighborhood, but it's much (interesting) _____more interesting_____.

2. Susan's sofa (fashionable) _____ her sister's sofa, but it's much (comfortable) _____.

3. These apartments (modern) _____ our apartment, but they're much (large) _____.

4. George's car (powerful) _____ Jack's car, but it's much (reliable) _____.

5. The weather in our city (warm) _____ the weather in your city, but it's much (sunny) _____.

6. My parents (talkative) _____ my cousin's parents, but they're much (understanding) _____.

7. The movie we rented last weekend wasn't (exciting) _____ this movie, but it was much (good) _____.

Q YOU'RE RIGHT

1. A. Ken's tie isn't as attractive as Len's tie.

   B. You're right. Len's tie is _____more_____ _____attractive than Ken's tie_____.

2. A. Donald isn't as nice as Ronald.

   B. You're right. Ronald is _____.

3. A. Larry isn't as lazy as his brother.

   B. You're right. Larry's brother is _____.

4. A. English isn't as difficult as Russian.

   B. You're right. Russian is _____.

5. A. Julie's office isn't as big as Judy's office.

   B. You're right. Judy's office is _____.

6. A. My son isn't as talkative as your son.

   B. You're right. My son is _____.

Listen. Then clap and practice.

Where's my   ticket?

Who has   mine?

I don't   want to

stand in   line.

Who has   hers?

Who has   his?

I wonder   where

my ticket   is!

He has   his.

I have   mine.

She has   hers.

Everything's   fine!

Listen. Then clap and practice.

His job is   easy.

Hers is,   too.

Mine's a more   difficult   job to   do.

His job's as   simple

As A B   C.

Mine   requires a   P h   D.

T WHO SHOULD WE HIRE?

A. Do you think we should hire Mr. Blake or Mr. Maxwell?

B. I'm not sure. Mr. Blake isn't as (lively) _____lively_____ [1]

as Mr. Maxwell, but he's much (smart) _____ [2].

A. I agree. Mr. Blake is very smart, but in my opinion,

Mr. Maxwell is (talented) _____ [3] than
Mr. Blake.

B. Well, perhaps Mr. Blake isn't as (talented) _____ [4] as

Mr. Maxwell, but I think he's probably (honest) _____ [5].

A. Do you really think so?

B. Yes. I think Mr. Blake is much (good) _____ [6] for the job.
We should hire him.

A. Do you think we should hire Ms. Taylor or Ms. Tyler?

B. I'm not sure. Ms. Tyler isn't as (friendly) _____ [7]

as Ms. Taylor, but I think she's much (intelligent) _____

_____ [8].

A. But Ms. Taylor is (talkative) _____ [9]

and (polite) _____ [10] than Ms. Tyler.

B. That's true. But I think Ms. Tyler is (capable) _____

_____ [11] than Ms. Taylor. I think we should hire her.

A. Do you think we should hire Mario or Victor?

B. I don't know. Mario's meatballs are (good) _____ [12]

than Victor's, but his desserts aren't as (delicious)

_____ [13] as Victor's desserts.

A. That's true. But Mario's vegetable stew is (interesting)

_____ [14] than Victor's. Also, Mario is

much (fast) _____ [15] than Victor. He's also

(nice) _____ [16] than Victor.

B. You're right. I think we should hire Mario.

will + be + verb + ing

1. A. I think Alice is very bright.

    B. She certainly is. She's ___the___

    ___brightest___ student in our class.

2. A. Your brother Tom is very neat.

    B. He certainly is. He's _____

    _____ person I know.

3. A. Our upstairs neighbors are very nice.

    B. I agree. They're _____
        people in the building.

4. A. This dress is very fancy.

    B. I know. It's _____
        dress in the store.

5. A. I think Nancy is very friendly.

    B. I agree. She's _____
        person in our office.

6. A. Timothy is very quiet.

    B. I know. He's _____
        boy in the school.

7. A. Is their new baby cute?

    B. In my opinion, she's _____

    _____ baby girl in
        the hospital.

8. A. That dog is very big.

    B. It certainly is. It's _____

    _____ dog in the
        neighborhood.

9. A. Your cousin Steven is very sloppy.

    B. He certainly is. He's _____

    _____ person I know.

10. A. Morton Miller is very mean.

    B. I agree. He's _____

    _____ man in town.

boring	generous	interesting	patient	smart	talented
energetic	honest	noisy	polite	stubborn	

1. Jessica sings, dances, and plays the guitar. She's very _____ talented _____.

   In fact, she's _____ the most talented _____ person I know.

2. Mr. Bates gives very expensive gifts to his friends. He's very _____.

   In fact, he's _____ person I know.

3. My Aunt Louise jogs every day before work. She's very _____.

   In fact, she's _____ person I know.

4. Marvin always says "Thank you" and "You're welcome." He's very _____.

   In fact, he's _____ person I know.

5. Samantha always knows the answers to all the questions. She's very _____.

   In fact, she's _____ person I know.

6. Edward isn't reading a very exciting novel. It's very _____.

   In fact, it's _____ book in his house.

7. Dr. Chen never gets angry. She's very _____.

   In fact, she's _____ person I know.

8. Mayor Jones always says what he thinks. He's very _____.

   In fact, he's _____ person I know.

9. My next-door neighbor plays loud music after midnight. He's very _____.

   In fact, he's _____ person I know.

10. I'm never bored in my English class. My English teacher is very _____.

    In fact, she's _____ person I know.

11. My brother-in-law is always sure he's right. He's very _____.

    In fact, he's _____ person I know.

C WORLDBUY.COM

WorldBuy.com is a very popular website on the Internet. People like to shop there because they can find wonderful products from around the world at very low prices.

1. *(attractive!)* Julie is buying a briefcase from Italy because she thinks that Italian briefcases are _____the most attractive_____ briefcases in the world.

2. *(soft!)* David is buying leather boots from Spain because he thinks that Spanish boots are _____ boots in the world.

3. *(elegant!)* Francine is buying an evening gown from Paris because she thinks that French evening gowns are _____ gowns in the world.

4. *(modern!)* Mr. and Mrs. Chang are buying a sofa from Sweden because they think that Swedish furniture is _____ furniture in the world.

5. *(warm!)* Victor is buying a fur hat from Russia because he thinks that Russian hats are _____ hats in the world.

6. *(good!)* Brenda is buying a sweater from England because she thinks that English sweaters are _____ sweaters in the world.

7. *(reliable!)* Michael is buying a watch from Switzerland because he thinks that Swiss watches are _____ watches in the world.

8. *(beautiful!)* Mr. and Mrs. Rivera are buying a rug from China because they think that Chinese rugs are _____ rugs in the world.

9. *(delicious!)* Nancy is buying coffee from Brazil because she thinks that Brazilian coffee is _____ in the world.

10. *(............!)* I'm buying .... from .... because I think that ....s is/are .... in the world.

Listen. Then clap and practice.

A. What do you think about Kirk?
B. He's the friendliest person at work!

A. What do you think about Flo?
B. She's the most patient person I know!

A. What do you think about Pete?
B. He's the nicest boy on the street!

A. What do you think about Kate?
B. She's the most talented teacher in the state!

A. What do you think about Bob?
B. He's the laziest guy on the job!

A. What do you think about Frank?
B. He's the most polite teller at the bank!

A. What do you think about Nellie?
B. She's the fastest waitress at the deli!

A. What do you think about this kitty?
B. It's the ugliest cat in the city!

THE BEST IN THE WORLD!

1. A. How do you like your new BMB van, Mr. Lopez?

    B. It's very powerful. It's much ___more___

    _____powerful_____ than my old van.

    A. That's because the BMB van is _____

    _____the most powerful_____ van in the world!

2. A. How do you like your Suny video camera, Mrs. Park?

    B. It's very lightweight. It's much _____

    _____ than my old video camera.

    A. That's because the Suny video camera is _____

    _____ video camera in the world!

3. A. How do you like your new Inkflo printer, Ted?

    B. It's very efficient. It's much _____

    _____ than my old printer.

    A. That's because the Inkflo printer is _____

    _____ printer in the world!

4. A. How do you like your Panorama fax machine, Jane?

    B. It's very dependable. It's much _____

    _____ than my old fax machine.

    A. That's because the Panorama fax machine is _____

    _____ fax machine in the world!

5. A. How do you like your new Ever-Lite Flashlight, Henry?

    B. It's very bright. It's much _____ than the
        flashlight I usually use.

    A. That's because the Ever-Lite Flashlight is _____

    _____ flashlight in the world!

Listen and circle the words you hear.

1. (more comfortable) the most comfortable
2. the best the worst
3. more energetic the most energetic
4. cheap cheaper
5. the most important more important

6. sloppier the sloppiest
7. the worst the best
8. lazier lazy
9. meaner mean
10. more honest the most honest

G PUZZLE

| boring | comfortable | delicious | good | honest | polite | safe | sloppy | small | ugly |

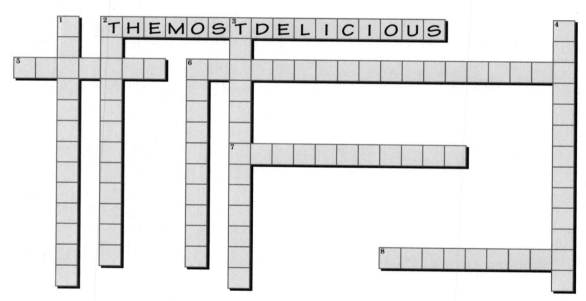

Across

2. Some people don't like this cereal. But I disagree. I think it's _____ cereal in the world.

5. Even though Harry's Restaurant is the most popular restaurant in town, it isn't _____.

6. This is my favorite chair. That's because it's _____ chair in the house.

7. My house isn't very big. In fact, it's _____ house on the street.

8. Their old neighborhood was dangerous, but their new neighborhood is _____ neighborhood in the city.

Down

1. Even though the salespeople at Ace Used Cars are the most helpful in town, they aren't _____.

2. My son isn't very neat. In my opinion, he's _____ person in our family.

3. I think golf is very interesting. But my wife disagrees. She thinks it's _____ game in the world.

4. Charles is never rude. In fact, he's _____ boy in the school.

6. Emily's cat isn't very pretty. In my opinion, it's _____ cat in town!

H **LOUD AND CLEAR** **r!**

Fill in the words. Then read the sentences aloud.

| worst | program | Andrew |
| terrible | | actor |

1. ___Andrew___ is the ___worst___ ___actor___ on this ___terrible___ TV ___program___!

| recipe | Carla's | fruitcake |
| recommend | | better |

2. I _____ _____ _____ for _____. It's _____ than yours.

| energetic | friendlier | Robert |
| more | | brother |

3. _____ is _____ and _____ _____ than his _____ Richard.

| newspaper | writes | reads |
| Rita | | morning |

4. _____ _____ the _____ every _____, and she _____ letters every afternoon.

| perfume | birthday | sister |
| Ronald | | thirtieth |

5. _____ gave his _____ flowers and _____ for her _____ _____.

| powerful | bigger | more |
| neighbor's | | car |

6. My _____ is _____ and _____ _____ than my _____ car.

A. Complete the sentences.

Ex. Will you be ready soon?

Yes, __I will__ . __I'll__
be ready in a few minutes.

Ex. Will your brother get home soon?

No, __he won't__ . He's at a baseball
game tonight.

1. Will the storm end soon?

Yes, _____ . _____
end in a few hours.

2. Will Carol and Dave be in the office today?

No, _____ . They're on vacation.

3. Will you return soon?

Yes, _____ . _____
return in a little while.

4. Will Jane be in school tomorrow?

No, _____ . She has a bad
cold.

5. Will you and Ray get out of work soon?

Yes, _____ . _____
get out in half an hour.

B. Circle the correct answers.

1. I'm not going to fix that wire. I'm

afraid I ⬚ might / should ⬚ get a shock.

2. What do you think?

⬚ Might / Should ⬚ I order the chicken or the fish?

3. When I grow up I ⬚ might / should ⬚ be a

dentist, or I ⬚ might / should ⬚ be a doctor.

4. It's going to rain. You ⬚ might / should ⬚ take

your umbrella.

C. Complete the conversations.

Ex. A. Are these Maria's gloves?

B. No. They aren't __hers__ .

1. A. Is that your video camera?

B. No. It isn't _____ .

2. A. Is that your son's computer?

B. No. It isn't _____ .

3. A. Is that Mr. and Mrs. Baker's house?

B. No. It isn't _____ .

4. A. Is this my recipe for meatballs?

B. No. It isn't _____ .

D. Fill in the blanks.

Ex. Donald is __neater than__ Sam.

neat

1. Jane is _____ Sarah.

tall

2. Carl is _____ Jack.

honest

3. Centerville is _____ Lakeville.

pretty

4. The pie is _____ the cake.

good

5. Julie is _____ John.

dependable

E. Complete the sentences.

Ex. William (rich) _____isn't as_____

_____rich as_____ Walter, but he's

much (happy) _____happier_____.

1. Ann's printer (fast) _____

_____ Betty's printer, but it's much

(reliable) _____ .

2. Danny's dog (friendly) _____

_____ Dorothy's dog, but it's much

(cute) _____ .

3. Howard (intelligent) _____

_____ Mike, but he's much (interesting)

_____ .

4. My apartment (fashionable) _____

_____ your

apartment, but it's much (big)

_____ .

5. Tom's furniture (expensive) _____

_____ John's

furniture, but it's much (attractive)

_____ .

F. Fill in the blanks.

Ex. Brian is _____the smartest_____ person

        smart

I know.

1. Marvin is _____ person

        quiet

I know.

2. Uncle Bert is _____

        hospitable

person in our family.

3. We have _____

        large

apartment in the building.

4. Mr. Peterson is _____

        patient

teacher in our school.

5. Mel is _____ person

        lazy

I know.

G. Listen and circle the correct answer.

Ex.

Ronald   Yes / No   Fred

1. Bob   Yes / No   Bill

    $6/lb.   Yes / No $4/lb.

2.

    Moscow   Yes / No   Miami

3. Moscow   Miami

4. Herbert   Yes / No   Steven

5. Pam   Yes / No   Patty

Activity Workbook   **59**

7

across from	on the right	walk up
between	on the left	walk down
next to		

SOUTH ST.

barber shop	library
clinic	toy store
shoe store	post office
bakery	book store
bank	drug store
high school	police station

1. A. Excuse me. Can you tell me how to get to the library from here?

   B. ___Walk up___ South Street and you'll see the library ___on the right___, ___across from___ the barber shop.

2. A. Excuse me. Can you tell me how to get to the clinic from here?

   B. _____ South Street and you'll see the clinic _____, _____ the shoe store.

3. A. Excuse me. Can you tell me how to get to the toy store from here?

   B. _____ South Street and you'll see the toy store _____, _____ the clinic.

4. A. Excuse me. Can you tell me how to get to the drug store from here?

   B. _____ South Street and you'll see the drug store _____, _____ the book store and the police station.

5. A. Excuse me. Can you tell me how to get to the high school from here?

   B. _____ South Street and you'll see the high school _____, _____ the bank and the police station.

B WHICH WAY?

across from
between
next to
on the left
on the right

walk along
walk down
walk up

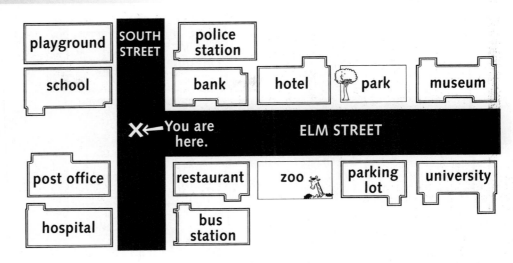

playground | SOUTH STREET | police station

school | bank | hotel | park | museum

X ← You are here. | ELM STREET

post office | restaurant | zoo | parking lot | university

hospital | bus station

1. A. Excuse me. Could you please tell me how to get to the university from here?

   B. ____Walk along____ Elm Street and you'll see the university

   ____on the right____ , ____across from____ the museum.

2. A. Excuse me. Could you please tell me how to get to the park from here?

   B. _____ Elm Street and you'll see the park

   _____ , _____ the hotel.

3. A. Excuse me. Could you please tell me how to get to the police station from here?

   B. _____ South Street and you'll see the police station

   _____ , _____ the playground.

4. A. Excuse me. Could you please tell me how to get to the bus station from here?

   B. _____ South Street and you'll see the bus station

   _____ , _____ the restaurant.

5. A. Excuse me. Could you please tell me how to get to the zoo from here?

   B. _____ Elm Street and you'll see the zoo

   _____ , _____ the restaurant and the parking lot.

Activity Workbook **61**

C LET'S HELP MR. AND MRS. LEE!

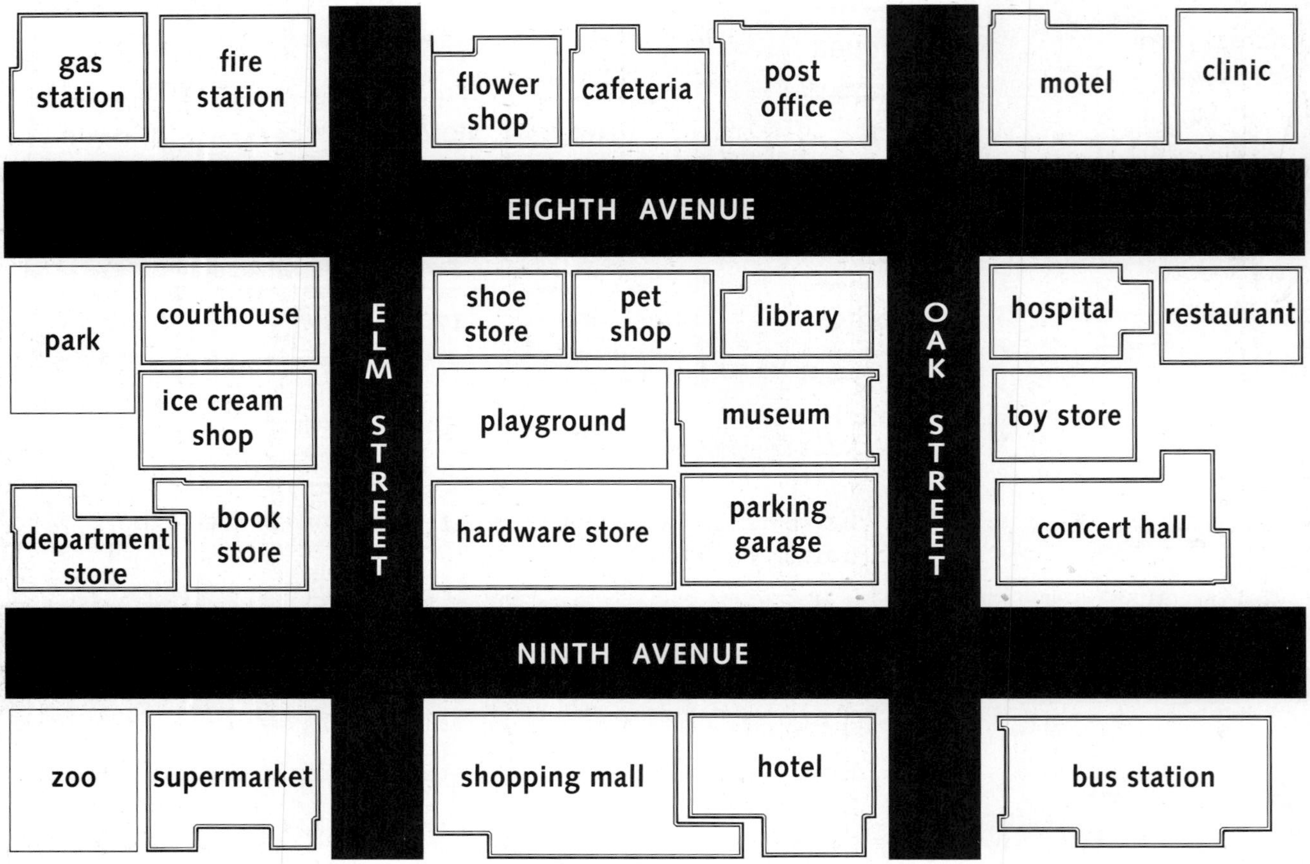

Mr. and Mrs. Lee are very busy today. They want to go several places with their children, but they don't know the city very well. They need your help.

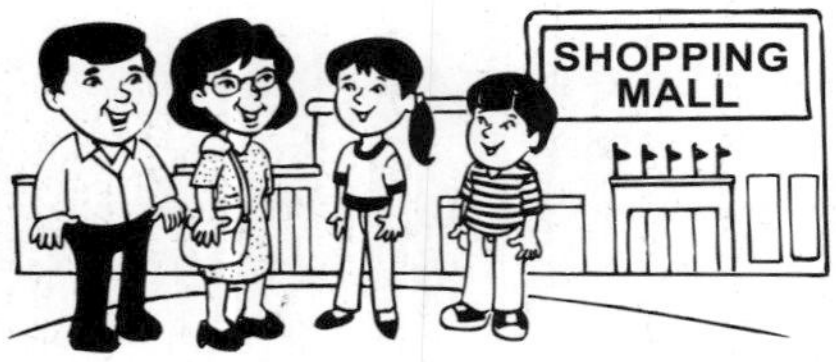

1. They're at the shopping mall, and they want to take their children to the toy store to buy them a new toy. Tell them how to get there.

> ___Walk along___ Ninth Avenue to Oak Street and ___turn left___. ___Walk up___ Oak Street and you'll see the toy store ___on the right___, ___across from___ the museum.

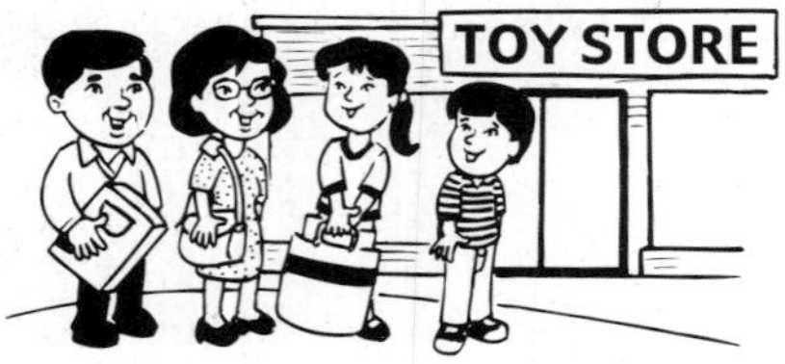

2. They're at the toy store, and now they want to take their children to the pet shop to buy them a dog.

> ____________ Oak Street to Eighth Avenue and ____________. ____________ Eighth Avenue and you'll see the pet shop ____________, ____________ the shoe store and the library.

3. They're at the pet shop, and they want to take their children to the ice cream shop for some ice cream.

_____ Eighth Avenue to Elm Street and _____. _____ Elm Street and you'll see the ice cream shop _____, _____ the courthouse.

4. They're at the ice cream shop, and they want to take their children to the zoo.

_____ Elm Street to Ninth Avenue and _____. _____ Ninth Avenue and you'll see the zoo _____, _____ the department store.

5. They're at the zoo, and they're tired. They want to go to the park to rest.

_____
_____
_____
_____

6. They had a wonderful day, and now it's time to go home. Tell them how to get to the bus station.

_____
_____
_____
_____

D **LISTENING**

Look at the map on page 62. Listen and choose the correct answer.

1. (a.) She was hungry.
    b.   She wanted to buy a bird.

2. a.   He wanted to look at paintings.
    b.   He wanted to listen to music.

3. a.   They wanted to read some books.
    b.   They wanted to buy some flowers.

4. a.   She wanted to buy some toys for her son.
    b.   She wanted to visit her sick friend.

5. a.   He wanted to buy some groceries.
    b.   He wanted to look at the animals.

6. a.   She was sick.
    b.   She was hungry.

E **GrammarRap:** *I Have a Terrible Sense of Direction*

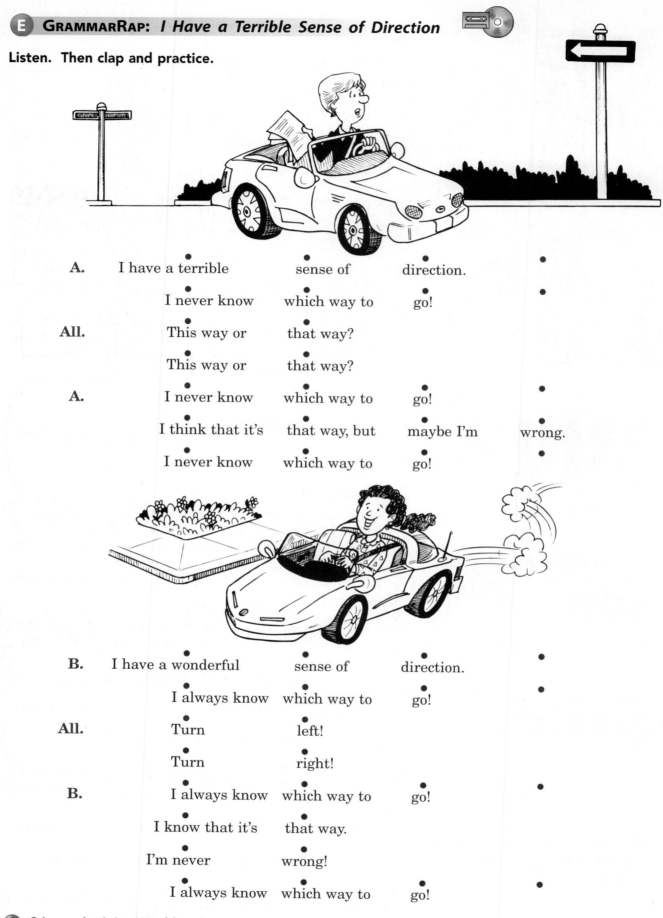

Listen. Then clap and practice.

A. I have a terrible   sense of   direction.
      I never know   which way to   go!

All. This way or   that way?
      This way or   that way?

A. I never know   which way to   go!
      I think that it's   that way, but   maybe I'm   wrong.
      I never know   which way to   go!

B. I have a wonderful   sense of   direction.
      I always know   which way to   go!

All. Turn   left!
      Turn   right!

B. I always know   which way to   go!
      I know that it's   that way.
      I'm never   wrong!
      I always know   which way to   go!

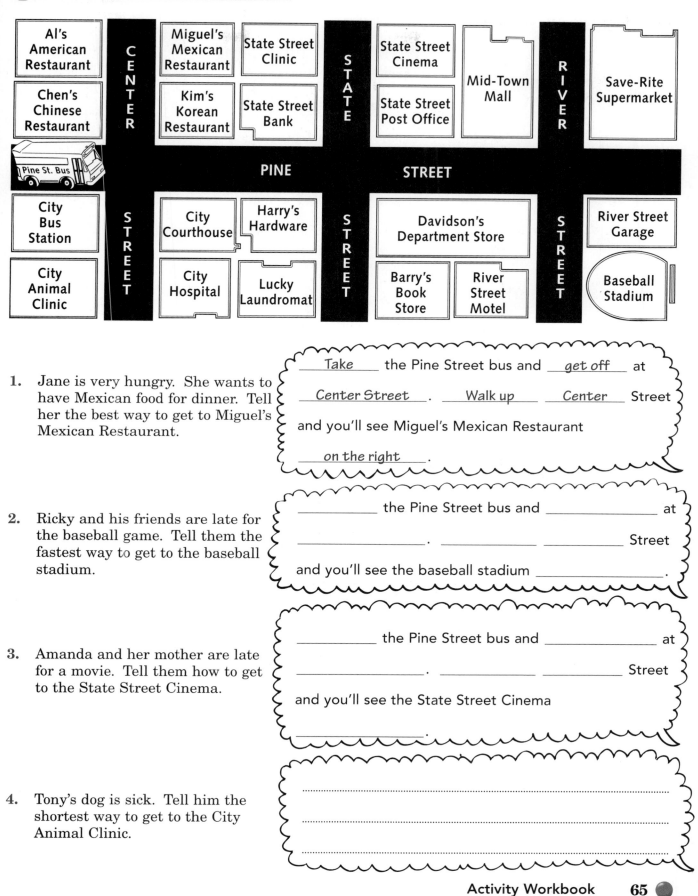

1. Jane is very hungry. She wants to have Mexican food for dinner. Tell her the best way to get to Miguel's Mexican Restaurant.

   ___Take___ the Pine Street bus and ___get off___ at ___Center Street___. ___Walk up___ ___Center___ Street and you'll see Miguel's Mexican Restaurant ___on the right___.

2. Ricky and his friends are late for the baseball game. Tell them the fastest way to get to the baseball stadium.

   _____ the Pine Street bus and _____ at _____. _____ _____ Street and you'll see the baseball stadium _____.

3. Amanda and her mother are late for a movie. Tell them how to get to the State Street Cinema.

   _____ the Pine Street bus and _____ at _____. _____ _____ Street and you'll see the State Street Cinema _____.

4. Tony's dog is sick. Tell him the shortest way to get to the City Animal Clinic.

Listen. Then clap and practice.

Which way do we · go?
Does anybody · know?
Which way do we · go · from here?
Is it very · near?
Is it very · far?
I wish I · knew · where I left my · car!
Which way do we · go?
Does anybody · know
how to get · home · from here?

H **GRAMMARRAP:** *Turn Right!*

Listen. Then clap and practice.

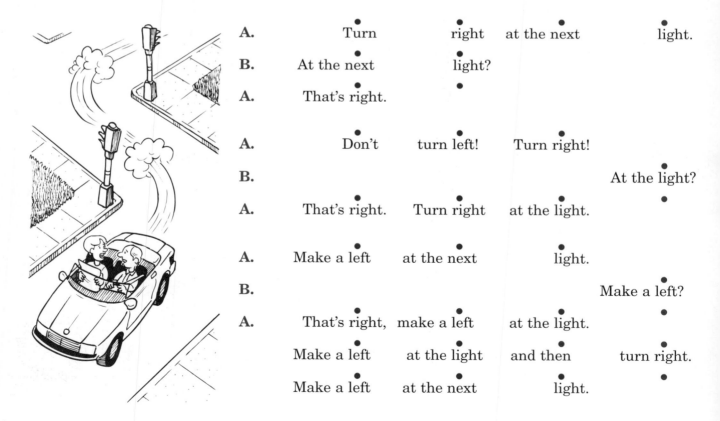

A.   Turn · right · at the next · light.
B.   At the next · light?
A.   That's right.

A.   Don't · turn left! · Turn right!
B.   At the light?
A.   That's right. · Turn right · at the light.

A.   Make a left · at the next · light.
B.   Make a left?
A.   That's right, · make a left · at the light.
Make a left · at the light · and then · turn right.
Make a left · at the next · light.

I LISTENING: *Where Did They Go?*

```
                        DAY STREET
┌─────────────────┐ F ┌─────────────────────┐ S ┌──────────────────────┐ T
│  shopping mall  │ I │       museum        │ E │       hospital       │ H
├────────┬────────┤ R ├──────┬──────┬───────┤ C ├────────┬───────┬─────┤ I
│ bakery │  bus   │ S │ ice  │motel │ clinic│ O │  high  │ post │park │ R
│        │station │ T │cream │      │       │ N │ school │office│     │ D
│        │  hotel │   │ shop │      │       │ D │        │      │     │
```

BRIGHTON BOULEVARD

| barber shop | book store | drug store | | parking lot | toy store | gas station | | police station | bank | pet shop |
| concert hall | | zoo | | flower shop | library | church | | shoe store | parking garage | fire station |

BAY AVENUE

Listen and fill in the correct places.

1. He went to the _____ bank _____ .

2. She went to the _____ .

3. They went to the _____ .

4. She went to the _____ .

5. They went to the _____ .

6. He went to the _____ .

J WHAT'S THE WORD?

| between | could | from | how | off | | subway | turn | walk |
| certainly | excuse | get | left | please | | take | up | |

A. _____Excuse_____ [1] me. _____ [2] you _____ [3]
tell me _____ [4] to _____ [5] to the train
station _____ [6] here?

B. _____ [7] . _____ [8] the
_____ [9] and get _____ [10] at Park Street.
Walk _____ [11] Park Street to Tenth Avenue
and _____ [12] right. _____ [13] along Tenth
Avenue and you'll see the train station on the
_____ [14] , _____ [15] the post office
and the fire station.

1. A. I think Barbara is a terrible dancer. What do you think?

   B. I agree. She dances _____terribly_____ .

2. A. Is Edward an accurate translator?

   B. He certainly is. He translates very _____.

3. A. I think Susan is a graceful swimmer.

   B. I agree. She swims very _____.

4. A. Is George a bad painter?

   B. Yes, he is. He paints very _____.

5. A. Is Rita a careful worker?

   B. Yes. She works very _____.

6. A. I think Fred is a dishonest card player.

   B. I agree. He plays cards very _____.

7. A. I think Roger is a careless skier.

   B. You're right. He skis very _____.

8. A. Your sister Jill is a very slow eater.

   B. I agree. She eats very _____.

9. A. Is Robert a _____ runner?

   B. Yes. He runs very fast.

10. A. I think Ron is a _____ skater.

    B. He certainly is. He skates very beautifully.

11. A. Is Margaret a _____ worker?

    B. Yes, she is. She works very hard.

12. A. I think Frank is a _____ baker.

    B. I agree. He bakes very well.

B ANSWER CAREFUL / CAREFULLY

1. Dr. Brown is a (careful / carefully) dentist. He cleans teeth very (careful / carefully) .

2. We play golf (terrible / terribly), but we're (good / well) soccer players.

3. Mark dances (beautiful / beautifully). He's very (graceful / gracefully) .

4. Richard isn't a very (good / well) driver. He drives very (fast / fastly) .

5. I usually skate (safe / safely), but I was very (careless / carelessly) yesterday.

6. Anna bakes pies very (bad / badly), but her family eats her pies (polite / politely) .

7. According to Sayako, you can't live (cheap / cheaply) in Tokyo. It's very (expensive / expensively) .

8. Everybody in the office likes Rick. He's (reliable / reliably), and he works (energetic / energetically) .

C LISTENING

Listen and circle the correct word to complete the sentence.

1. (slow)   slowly   5. accurate   accurately   9. soft   softly

2. beautiful   beautifully   6. rude   rudely   10. cheap   cheaply

3. dishonest   dishonestly   7. safe   safely   11. careful   carefully

4. sloppy   sloppily   8. reliable   reliably   12. patient   patiently

D GRAMMARRAP: *How Am I Doing?*

Listen. Then clap and practice.

A.   How am I   doing?

      Am I driving   all right?

B.   You're driving very   carefully.

      You're driving very   well.

A.   How am I   doing?

      Am I singing   all right?

B.   You're singing very   beautifully.

      You're singing very   well.

A.   How am I   doing?

      Am I dancing   all right?

B.   You're dancing very   gracefully.

      You're dancing very   well.

A.   How am I   doing?

      Am I working   all right?

B.   You're working very   hard.

      You're working very   well.

1. A. Am I jogging fast enough?
   B. You should try to jog

   faster .

2. A. Harold isn't speaking loudly enough.
   B. I agree. He should speak

   .

3. A. Am I typing carefully enough?
   B. Actually, you should type

   .

4. A. Is he translating accurately enough?
   B. No, he isn't. He should translate

   .

5. A. Rob, I don't think you're doing your work quickly enough.
   B. I'm sorry. I'll try to do my work

   .

6. A. I know I'm not dancing gracefully enough.
   B. You're right. You should dance

   .

7. A. Am I cleaning the office well enough?
   B. Actually, you should clean it

   .

8. A. Is the new mechanic working hard enough?
   B. I think he should work

   .

9. A. Amanda, be careful! You aren't driving slowly enough!

   B. I'm sorry, Mr. Sanders. I'll try to drive _____.

RALPH SHOULD TRY HARDER!

Ralph has some problems. What should he do to make his life better?

1. Ralph always gets up very late.

   He should try to get up _____earlier_____.

2. He sometimes dresses very sloppily.

   He should try to dress _____.

3. He always eats breakfast very quickly.

   He should try to eat _____.

4. He sometimes speaks rudely on the bus.

   He should try to speak _____.

5. He usually works very slowly.

   He should try to work _____.

6. He sometimes types carelessly.

   He should try to type _____.

7. He plays his CD player very loudly every night.

   He should try to play it _____.

G **WHAT SHOULD *YOU* TRY TO DO BETTER?**

I should try to ....

I should try to ....

I should try to ....

I should try to ....

Listen and circle the words to the song. Then listen again and sing along.

Let's say you're a driver, a (careful) / carefully [1] driver who

drives very careful / carefully [2] , as careful / carefully [3] drivers do.

Just try a little harder. You can find a way. Try to drive more careful / carefully [4] today.

Let's say you're a singer, a beautiful / beautifully [5] singer who

sings very beautiful / beautifully [6] , as beautiful / beautifully [7] singers do.

Just try a little harder. You can find a way. Try to sing more beautiful / beautifully [8] today.

Let's say you're a dancer, a graceful / gracefully [9] dancer who

dances very graceful / gracefully [10] , as graceful / gracefully [11] dancers do.

Try a little harder. You can find a way. Try to dance more graceful / gracefully [12] today.

Just try a little harder. That's what we always say. Sing a little strong / stronger [13]. Work a little

long / longer [14]. Do a little good / better [15] every day. Do a little good / better [16] every day.

I WHAT'S THE ANSWER?

1. If Helen _____ sick tomorrow, she'll go to work.
   - (a.) isn't
   - b. won't be

2. If the mechanic at Al's Garage fixes our car, _____ to the beach.
   - a. we drive
   - b. we'll drive

3. If _____ to your grandparents, they'll be very happy.
   - a. you write
   - b. you'll write

4. If Betty doesn't buy a VCR, _____ a CD player.
   - a. she buys
   - b. she'll buy

5. If you don't use enough butter, the cake _____ very good.
   - a. isn't
   - b. won't be

6. If _____ a course with Professor Boggs, I know it'll be boring.
   - a. I take
   - b. I'll take

7. If it _____ this Saturday, I think I'll go skiing.
   - a. snows
   - b. will snow

8. If you send me an e–mail, _____ right away.
   - a. I answer
   - b. I'll answer

9. If you _____ any more potatoes, I'll have rice with my chicken.
   - a. don't have
   - b. won't have

10. If the weather _____ good tomorrow, we'll play tennis.
    - a. is
    - b. will be

11. If I go on the roller coaster with you, I know _____ sick.
    - a. I get
    - b. I'll get

12. If you go there on your vacation, I'm sure _____ a good time.
    - a. you have
    - b. you won't have

J MATCHING

_d_	1. If you stay on the beach all day,	a. you won't get hurt.
___	2. If you use fresh oranges,	b. you'll be hungry.
___	3. If you wear safety glasses,	c. you won't get lost.
___	4. If you follow my directions to the zoo,	d. you'll get a sunburn.
___	5. If you don't eat breakfast,	e. you'll get the job.
___	6. If you have a successful interview,	f. the juice will be better.

K IF

1. If we _____arrive_____ early, _____we'll_____ visit your mother.

2. If _____ this afternoon, I'll wear my new raincoat.

3. If the weather _____ good, my husband and I _____ sailing.

4. If David _____ golf this weekend, _____ a wonderful time.

5. If you _____ a lot of noise, your neighbors _____ upset.

6. If your son _____ those wires, _____ a shock.

7. If _____ cold this Saturday, our family _____ skiing.

8. If Patty _____ too much candy, _____ a stomachache.

9. If I _____ too many exercises, _____ tired tonight.

10. If we _____ a girl, _____ her Patty.

11. If _____ a lot of traffic this morning, Nancy _____ probably be late for work.

12. If your parents _____ to Stanley's Restaurant on Monday, _____ _____ Italian food.

L SCRAMBLED SENTENCES

1. to   suit.   If   he   he'll   party,   goes   new   his   the   wear

   _____If he goes to the party_____ , _____he'll wear his new suit_____ .

2. late   she   work.   she'll   be   If   bus,   the   misses   for

   _____ , _____ .

3. better.   practice,   I   chess   play   I'll   If

   _____ , _____ .

4. buy   go   I   I'll   pie.   an   If   bakery,   the   apple   to

   _____ , _____ .

5. you   sorry.   If   finish   school,   be   you'll   don't

   _____ , _____ .

6. Sam   a   works   job.   in   good   If   he'll   hard   get   school,

   _____ , _____ .

M YOU DECIDE

Complete the sentences any way you wish.

1. If the weather is bad this weekend, ...

2. If I go to bed very late tonight, ...

3. If I don't eat dinner today, ...

4. If my computer breaks, ...

5. If I make a terrible mistake at school or at work, ...

6. If ...., they'll go to a special restaurant tonight.

7. If ...., his mother will be very happy.

8. If ...., his parents will be sad.

9. If ...., his boss will fire him.

10. If ...., my friends will be angry with me.

N GRAMMARRAP: *If You Leave at Six*

Listen. Then clap and practice.

If you leave at   six,
You'll be there at   eight.
If you don't leave   now,
You'll be very   late.

If you start work   now,
You'll be through at   seven.
If you wait 'till   noon,
You'll be busy 'till   eleven.

If you catch the   train,
You'll be home by   ten.
If you get there   late,
You'll miss dinner   again.

O YOU DECIDE: *What Might Happen?*

1. You shouldn't worry so much.

   If you worry too much, you might ....

2. Charlie shouldn't do his work so carelessly.

   If he does his work too carelessly, he might ....

3. Harriet shouldn't go to bed so late.

   If she goes to bed too late, she might ....

4. Your friends shouldn't use the Internet so much.

   If they use the Internet too much, they might ....

5. You shouldn't talk so much.

   If ...., ...

6. Veronica shouldn't eat so much.

   If ...., ...

7. Brian shouldn't buy so many expensive clothes.

   If ...., ...

8. Your friends shouldn't play their music so loud.

   If ...., ...

9. Raymond shouldn't speak so impolitely to his boss.

   If ...., ...

10. You shouldn't speak so loudly.

    If ...., ...

A. Please don't send me a lot of e-mail messages today!

B. Why not?

A. If you send me a lot of e-mail messages today, I'll have to read them tonight.

If ___*I have to read*___ [1] them tonight, _____*I'll*_____ [2] be tired tomorrow morning.

And if _____ [3] tired tomorrow morning, I'll fall asleep at work.

If _____ [4] at work, my boss _____ [5] be

understanding, and _____ [6] shout at me.

So please don't send me too many e-mail messages today!

A. Please don't play your CD player so loud!

B. Why not?

A. If you play your CD player too loud, the neighbors will be upset.

If _____ [7] upset, they'll tell the landlord.

And if _____ [8] the landlord, _____ [9] get angry.

So please don't play your CD player so loud!

A. Please don't buy Jimmy a scary video!

B. Why not?

A. If you buy him a scary video, _____ [10] be afraid when he

goes to sleep. If _____ [11] afraid when he goes to sleep,

_____ [12] have nightmares all night. If _____ [13]

nightmares all night, he _____ [14] get up on time. If

_____ [15] get up on time, _____ [16] late

for school. And if _____ [17] late for school, _____ [18]

miss a big test. So please don't buy Jimmy a scary video!

A. Complete the sentences.

Ex. She's a beautiful singer.

She sings very ___beautifully___ .

1. He's a terrible tennis player.

He plays tennis _____ .

2. She's a careful driver.

She drives very _____ .

3. They're bad cooks.

They cook very _____ .

4. I'm a hard worker.

I work very _____ .

B. Circle the correct answers.

1. He isn't an | honest / honestly | player.

He plays | dishonest / dishonestly | .

2. The bus is | quick / quickly | , but it isn't

| quiet / quietly | .

3. Mario is a | good / well | soccer player,

but he doesn't run very | good / well | .

4. Alice usually drives | safe / safely | , but

last night she was | careless / carelessly | .

C. Complete the sentences.

Ex. Timothy talks too quickly.
He should try to talk ___{ slower / more slowly }___ .

1. Greta leaves work too early.

She should try to leave work

_____ .

2. Bobby speaks too impolitely at school.

He should try to speak _____

_____ .

3. Linda dances too awkwardly.

She should try to dance _____

_____ .

4. Frank talks too softly.

He should try to talk _____ .

D. Complete the sentences.

Ex. If Jack ___does___ his homework, his

teacher ___will be___ happy.

1. If you _____ too many cookies,

_____ get a stomachache.

2. If the music _____ too loud,

the neighbors _____ angry.

3. If they _____ a boy,

_____ him Steven.

4. If _____ hungry tonight,
I'll eat a small dinner.

(continued)

E. Circle the correct answers.

1. If [we take / we'll take] a vacation this

   year, [we go / we'll go] to Hawaii.

2. If they [feel / will feel] energetic tonight,

   they [go / might go] dancing.

3. If you sing too loudly, you

   [get / might get] a sore throat.

4. If it [won't / doesn't] rain tomorrow,

   [I go / I'll go] sailing.

F. Listen and fill in the correct places.

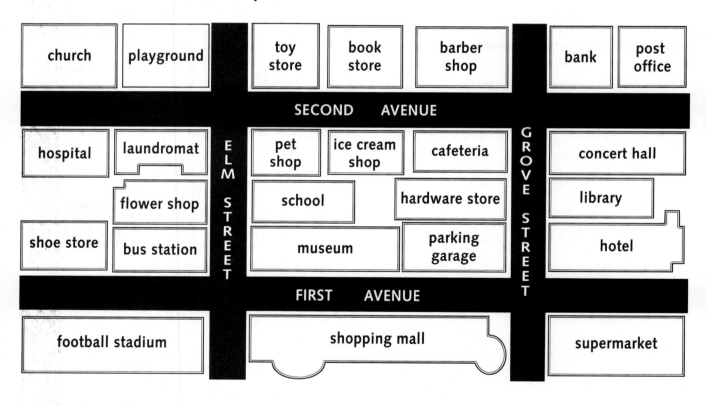

1. She went to the _____.

2. He went to the _____.

3. They went to the _____.

4. He went to the _____.

5. She went to the _____.

A WHAT WERE THEY DOING?

driving to the beach	playing basketball
fixing her fence	riding his motorcycle
jogging	skateboarding
painting their house	walking down Main Street

1. What was Paul doing when it started to rain?

   He was driving to the beach.

2. What was Diane doing when it started to rain?

   _____

3. What were Mr. and Mrs. Adams doing?

   _____

4. What were you and your friends doing?

   _____

5. What was Nick doing?

   _____

6. What was Natalie doing?

   _____

7. What were Tony and Mary doing?

   _____

8. What were you and Mike doing?

   _____

9. What were YOU doing?

   _____

B WHAT WERE THEY DOING?

1. My children (bake) ___were baking___ a cake when I got home from work.

2. He (wear) _____ a helmet when he hit his head.

3. They (play) _____ tennis when it started to rain.

4. She (ride) _____ on a roller coaster when she got sick.

5. We (watch) _____ a movie when we fell asleep.

6. He (sleep) _____ at his desk when his boss fired him.

7. They (have) _____ an argument when the guests arrived.

8. I (chat) _____ online when the lights went out.

9. She (talk) _____ to her friend when the teacher asked her a question.

C GRAMMARRAP: *Standing Around*

Listen. Then clap and practice.

We were singing and dancing and standing around,
Laughing and talking and standing around.

Susan was singing.
Danny was dancing.
Stella and Stanley were standing around.

Lucy was laughing.
Tommy was talking.
Stuart and Steven were standing around.

We were singing and dancing and standing around,
Laughing and talking and standing around.

D THE WRONG DAY!

Alan and his wife were very embarrassed when they arrived
at the Franklins' house yesterday. They thought the
Franklins' party was on Friday. But the Franklins' party
wasn't on Friday. It was on Saturday!

bake	clean	make	sweep	vacuum	wash

1. What was Mr. Franklin doing when
   they arrived?

   _____He was cleaning_____ the dining room.

2. What was Mrs. Franklin doing when
   they arrived?

   _____ the living room rug.

3. What was Tommy Franklin doing?

   _____ the kitchen floor.

4. What was his sister Lucy doing?

   _____ the windows.

5. What were Mrs. Franklin's parents doing?

   _____ spaghetti.

6. What were Mr. Franklin's parents doing?

   _____ cakes and cookies.

E LISTENING

Listen and choose the correct answer.

1. a. He was shaving.
   b. He was shopping.

2. a. She was skateboarding.
   b. She was skating.

3. a. They were sitting on the beach.
   b. They were swimming at the beach.

4. a. He was studying math.
   b. He was taking a bath.

5. a. We were reading.
   b. We were eating.

6. a. She was talking with her mother.
   b. She was walking with her brother.

7. a. He was taking a shower.
   b. He was planting flowers.

8. a. I was sleeping in the living room.
   b. I was sweeping the living room.

1. When I saw her, she was getting

   on
   off
   (into)

   a taxi on Main Street.

2. Al was walking

   out of
   off
   of

   the park when

   he fell.

3. I got

   from
   off
   up

   the bus and walked to

   the bank.

4. We went

   into
   out of
   at

   a restaurant because

   we were hungry.

5. Get

   at
   up
   on

   the subway at

   Sixth Avenue.

6. Ann was skating

   through
   along
   in

   Center Street.

7. I'm getting

   out of
   off
   up

   the car

   because I'm sick.

8. Susie got

   off
   to
   at

   the

   merry-go-round.

Listen and put the number under the correct picture.

_____

_____

_____

_____

_____

_____

1

_____

Listen. Then clap and practice.

A. I called you all day today,

But you never answered your phone.

B. That's strange! I was here from morning 'till night.

I was home all day all alone.

A. What were you doing when I called at nine?

B. I was probably hanging my clothes on the line.

A. What were you doing when I called at one?

B. I was probably sitting outside in the sun.

A. What were you doing when I called at four?

B. I was painting the hallway and fixing the door.

A. What were you doing when I called at six?

B. I was washing the dog to get rid of his ticks.

A. Well, I'm sorry I missed you when I tried to phone.

B. It's too bad. I was here. I was home all alone.

myself	yourself	himself	herself	ourselves	yourselves	themselves

1. Nobody wants to go fishing with me.

    I'll have to go fishing by _____myself_____.

2. Nobody wants to drive to the beach with her.

    She'll have to drive to the beach by _____.

3. Nobody wants to go to the circus with us.

    We'll have to go to the circus by _____.

4. Nobody wants to go to the playground with you.

    You'll have to go to the playground by _____.

5. Nobody wants to eat lunch with them.

    They'll have to eat lunch by _____.

6. Nobody wants to watch the video with him.

    He'll have to watch the video by _____.

7. Nobody wants to play volleyball with you and your brother.

    You'll have to play volleyball by _____.

J WHAT'S THE WORD?

1. My husband and I like to have a picnic by _____.
    (a.) ourselves
    b. ourself

2. Bobby likes to drink his milk by _____.
    a. hisself
    b. himself

3. My mother and father drove to the mountains by _____.
    a. themself
    b. themselves

4. My grandmother likes to take a walk in the park by _____.
    a. herself
    b. herselves

5. I like to do my homework by _____.
    a. myself
    b. yourself

6. You and your brother like to fix the car by _____.
    a. yourself
    b. yourselves

bite	cook	drop	fall	have	lose	ride		shave	steal	walk
burn	cut	faint	get on	hurt	paint	roller-blade	ski		trip	watch

1. Jane ____tripped____ while ____she____ _____was walking_____ down the stairs.

2. A dog _____ Johnny while _____ _____ his bicycle.

3. Sam _____ while _____ _____ a scary video.

4. Someone _____ our car while _____ _____ dinner at a restaurant.

5. Diane _____ her packages while _____ the bus.

6. I _____ myself while _____ _____.

7. Mr. and Mrs. Ling _____ themselves while _____ on the barbecue.

8. Brian _____ his wallet while _____.

9. We _____ ourselves while _____.

10. A can of paint _____ on them while _____ their house.

1. We were walking | through / into / (up) | the stairs.

2. They were driving | out of / over / down | a bridge.

3. A heavy book fell | on / out of / along | me.

4. They were walking | on / along / out of | the bank.

5. She was working | into / at / over | her office.

6. Let's go jogging | through / along / over | the park!

7. Don't walk | under / over / in | a ladder!

M LISTENING

Listen and choose the correct answer.

1. a. She lost her new boot.
   b. She lost her new suit.

2. a. He hurt himself while he was cooking.
   b. He burned himself while he was cooking.

3. a. While they were walking into the bank.
   b. While they were walking out of the park.

4. a. Someone stole our new fan.
   b. Someone stole our new van.

5. a. I dropped my new CD player.
   b. I dropped my new DVD player.

6. a. A dog bit him while he was working.
   b. A dog bit him while he was walking.

7. a. We were driving under a bridge.
   b. We were driving over a bridge.

8. a. She tripped and fell on the kitchen floor.
   b. She tripped and fell near the kitchen door.

9. a. While they were walking down the stairs.
   b. While they were walking up the stairs.

10. a. She was cooking on the barbecue.
    b. She was walking on Park Avenue.

11. a. I cut myself while I was chopping.
    b. I cut myself while I was shopping.

12. a. He waited at the bus stop.
    b. He fainted at the bus stop.

Listen. Then clap and practice.

A. Does she need a   ladder?   B.   No,   she doesn't.

She can reach the top   shelf by   herself.

All. She can reach the top   shelf by   herself.   Look at that!

She can reach the top   shelf by   herself!

A. Does he need a   cart?   B.   No,   he doesn't.

He can carry all the   luggage by   himself.

All. He can carry all the   luggage by   himself.   Look at that!

He can carry all the   luggage by   himself!

A. Do you need a   calculator?   B.   No,   I don't.

I can add all these   numbers by   myself.

All. You can add all those   numbers by   yourself.   Look at that!

You can add all those   numbers by   yourself!

LOUD AND CLEAR he! him!

Fill in the words. Then read the sentences aloud.

e-mail	Greece	reading
niece	keypal	

1. My ___niece___ Louise is _____

   an _____ from her _____

   in _____ .

himself	building	William	his
tripped	office		

2. _____ _____ and hurt

   _____ in front of _____

   _____ _____ .

cheese	asleep	fifteen	cookies
Steve	three		

3. _____ fell _____ at _____

   _____ . He ate too many _____

   and too much _____ .

busy	children	Hill	sick
clinic	city		

4. Dr. _____ is very _____ at his

   _____ . A lot of _____

   in the _____ are _____ today.

beach	she's	Lee	Tahiti
CDs	sleeping		

5. Mr. and Mrs. _____ are on the _____

   in _____ . He's _____ , and

   _____ listening to _____ .

sandwich	isn't	milk	little
spilled	sister		

6. My _____ _____ Jill _____

   very happy. She dropped her _____

   and _____ her _____ .

90

WHAT'S THE WORD?

could	can
couldn't	can't

10

1. Before I took lessons from Mrs. Rossini, I _____*couldn't*_____ play the violin very well.

   Now I _____*can*_____ play the violin beautifully.

2. I'm sorry you _____ go to the beach with us last weekend. Maybe you

   _____ go with us next weekend.

3. When I first arrived in this country, I was frustrated because I _____ speak

   English. Now I'm happy because I _____ speak English very well.

4. We _____ hear him because he spoke too softly.

5. We really want to fire Howard, but we _____. His father is president of the
   company.

6. My parents tell me that I was a very bright little girl. According to them, I_____

   read when I was two years old, and I _____ write when I was three years old.

7. We _____ move the refrigerator by ourselves because it was too heavy.

8. I _____ go to work yesterday because I was sick. But today I'm feeling much

   better. I'm sure I _____ go to work tomorrow.

9. Michael _____go to lunch with his co-workers because he was too busy.

10. I _____ play basketball when I was in high school because I was too short. But

   I wasn't upset because I _____ play on the baseball team.

11.
    I'm disappointed. We _____ barbecue tonight. It's raining.

12.
    I _____ ask my boss for a raise. I was too nervous.

Listen. Then clap and practice.

A.   She tried on the skirt, but she   couldn't zip it   up.

B.   Was it too   small?

A.   Much too   small.

A.   She tried on the shoes, but she   couldn't keep them   on.

B. Were they too   big?

A.   Much too   big.

A.   He tried to   talk, but he   couldn't say a   word.

B.   Was he too   nervous?

A.   Much too   nervous.

A.   She sat at the   table, but she   couldn't eat a   thing.

B.   Was she too   excited?

A.   Much too   excited.

A.   He went to the   lecture, but he   couldn't stay   awake.

B.   Was he too   tired?

A.   Much too   tired.

A.   She took the   course, but she   couldn't pass the   test.

B.   Was it too   hard?

A.   Much too   hard.

C YOU DECIDE: *Why Weren't They Able to?*

wasn't able to	weren't able to

1. Daniel _____wasn't able to_____ lift the package

because _____it was too heavy_____ (*or*)

_____he was too tired_____ (*or*)

_____he was too weak._____

2. Barbara _____ go to work yesterday because _____

_____

3. My grandparents _____ finish their dinner because _____

_____

4. Jim _____ buy the car he wanted because _____

_____

5. I _____ get on the bus this morning because _____

_____

6. The students in my class _____ solve the puzzle because _____

_____

7. Maria _____ fall asleep last night because _____

_____

8. My brother _____ wear my tuxedo to his wedding because _____

_____

9. We _____ go sailing last weekend because _____

_____

10. Robert _____ say "I love you" to his girlfriend because _____

_____

could was/were able to	couldn't wasn't/weren't able to	had to

1. The bus was very crowded this morning. I ___couldn't / wasn't able to___ sit. I ___had to___ stand.

2. Carlos was very disappointed. He _____ take his daughter to the circus on Saturday because he _____ work overtime.

3. When I was young, I was very energetic. I _____ run five miles every day.

4. When Judy was ten years old, her family moved to a different city. She was sad because she _____ see her old friends very often.

5. When I was a little boy, I was upset because my older brothers _____ go to bed late, but I _____. I _____ go to bed at 7:30 every night.

6. We're sorry we _____ go to the tennis match with you yesterday. We _____ take our car to the mechanic.

7. When I was a teenager, I was very athletic. I _____ play baseball, and I _____ play football. But I was a terrible singer and dancer. I _____ sing, and I _____ dance.

8. My wife and I _____ go to our son's soccer game after school yesterday because we _____ meet with our lawyer.

9. Brian was upset because he wanted to have long hair, but he _____. He _____ go to the barber every month because his parents liked very short hair.

YOU DECIDE: *Why Didn't They Enjoy Themselves?*

myself	ourselves		couldn't
yourself	yourselves		wasn't able to
himself	themselves		weren't able to
herself			

1. I didn't enjoy _____myself_____ at the beach yesterday.

   It was very windy, and I ____couldn't go swimming____ (*or*)

   _____wasn't able to go sailing_____

2. Jim and his friends didn't enjoy _____ at the movie yesterday. It was

   very scary, and they _____

3. Nancy didn't enjoy _____ at the museum. It was very crowded, and she

   _____

4. Edward didn't enjoy _____ at the restaurant last night. The food was

   very spicy, and he _____

5. I didn't enjoy _____ at the circus last Friday. It was very noisy, and I

   _____

6. We didn't enjoy _____ on our vacation last winter. We got sick, and we

   _____

F **WHAT'S THE WORD?**

1. Walter was pleased. He didn't have to call the plumber. He ____ fix the sink himself.
   a. couldn't
   b. was able to *(circled)*

2. I ____ get to work on time this morning because the bus was late.
   a. was able to
   b. couldn't

3. I missed the company picnic yesterday because I ____ go to the eye doctor.
   a. had to
   b. wasn't able to

4. We ____ finish our dinner because we were too full.
   a. could
   b. weren't able to

5. I forgot my briefcase, and I ____ to go back home and get it.
   a. wasn't able to
   b. had

6. We ____ fall asleep last night. Our neighbors played their music very loudly.
   a. couldn't
   b. were able to

| I've | she's | they've | got to |
| he's | we've | you've | |

Tomorrow afternoon David is moving to a new apartment next door. He asked a lot of people to help him, but unfortunately, everybody is busy tomorrow afternoon, and nobody will be able to help him. They all have things they've got to do.

1. His friend Bob won't be able to help him.

   _____He's got to_____ take his daughter to the doctor.

2. His friend Sandra won't be able to help him.

   _____ drive her brother to the train station.

3. I'm sorry. I won't be able to help you.

   _____ take care of my neighbor's little boy.

4. Tom and I won't be able to help you, either.

   _____ stay home and wait for the plumber.

5. David's brother won't be able to help him.

   _____ study for an important English test.

6. David's cousins won't be able to help him.

   _____ go to baseball practice.

7. We're really sorry, David.

   Unfortunately, _____ move to your new apartment by yourself.

H MY FRIEND LISA

> will / won't be able to

My friend Lisa is an active, energetic person.

1. She goes jogging every morning.
2. She rides her bicycle to school every day.
3. She plays tennis on the school team.
4. She swims every afternoon.
5. She does exercises every evening.

She's also very talented and capable.

6. She plays the violin.
7. She bakes delicious cakes and cookies.
8. She makes her own clothes.
9. She fixes her computer when it's broken.

Last week on Friday the 13th Lisa went skating, and unfortunately, she broke her leg. The doctor says she'll have to rest her leg all month. Lisa is very upset.

1. _____She won't be able to go jogging every morning._____

2. _____

3. _____

4. _____

5. _____

Fortunately, there are many things that Lisa WILL be able to do.

6. _____She'll be able to play the violin._____

7. _____

8. _____

9. _____

I THEY'LL BE ABLE TO

> couldn't   will be able to

1. My daughter ____couldn't____ go to her ballet lesson today, but I'm sure ___she'll be able to___ go next week.

2. We _____ assemble our new lamp yesterday. I hope _____ assemble it today.

3. Bill _____ go to football practice today. He thinks _____ go to football practice tomorrow.

4. I _____ fall asleep last night. I hope _____ fall asleep tonight.

THEY WON'T BE ABLE TO

won't be able to	have/has got to

1. I'm sorry. I _____ won't be able to _____ cook dinner tonight.

   _____ I've got to _____ work overtime.

2. I'm terribly sorry. My daughter _____ baby-sit

   this afternoon. _____ practice the violin.

3. My children _____ eat ice cream at the party.

   Their doctor told them_____ eat fruit for dessert.

4. I'm really upset. My father _____ lend us money

   because _____ buy a new van.

5. Unfortunately, my husband and I _____ play golf

   with you today. _____ take our dog to the vet.

K **LISTENING**

Listen to each story, and then choose the correct answers to the questions you hear.

William's New Apartment

1. a. He was able to open his living room windows.
   b. He couldn't open his living room windows.

2. a. The lights in his apartment went out.
   b. His apartment is too bright.

3. a. He won't be able to cook dinner.
   b. He'll be able to watch his favorite programs on TV.

Mr. and Mrs. Clark's New Computer

4. a. They could assemble their computer easily.
   b. They weren't able to assemble their computer easily.

5. a. Their computer crashed.
   b. They used their new computer.

6. a. They'll be able to call their grandchildren.
   b. They won't be able to send any e-mail to their grandchildren.

L GRAMMARRAP: *Were You Able to?*

Listen. Then clap and practice.

A. Were you able to leave early last night?

B. No. I had to work until seven.

A. Were you able to get to the office on time?

B. No. I couldn't get there 'till eleven.

A. Were you able to take the six o'clock bus?

B. No. I had to wait until eight.

A. Were you able to get to the meeting on time?

B. No. I had to walk in late.

M GRAMMARRAP: *They Won't Be Able to*

Listen. Then clap and practice.

A. Will you be able to join us for dinner?

B. No, I won't. I've got to work late.

A. Will he be able to meet us tomorrow?

B. No, he won't. He's got to see Kate.

A. Will she be able to come to the meeting?

B. No, she won't. She's got to call Jack.

A. Will they be able to go on the sightseeing trip?

B. No, they won't. They've got to unpack.

Activity Workbook   **99**

GrammarSong: *I'm Afraid I Won't Be Able to*

Listen and fill in the words to the song. Then listen again and sing along.

| day | do | go | no | play | to | today |

My friend Jim called the other ___*day*___ 1.

He said, "Would you like to see a play _____ 2?"

I didn't really want to _____ 3, so this is how I told him _____ 4.

I'm afraid I won't be able _____ 5. I have a lot of things to _____ 6.

I've got to wash my clothes and clean my house today.

But thank you for the invitation. I want to express my appreciation.

I'm sure that we'll be able to see a _____ 7 another _____ 8.

My friend Bob called the other _____ 9.

He said, "Would you like to roller-skate _____ 10?"

I didn't really want to _____ 11, so this is how I told him _____ 12.

I'm afraid I won't be able _____ 13. I have a lot of things to _____ 14.

I've got to paint my house and bathe my cat today.

But thank you for the invitation. I want to express my appreciation.

I'm sure that we'll be able to roller-skate another day.

I'm sure that we'll be able to.

I'm sure that we'll be able to.

A. Complete the sentences.

Ex. She (wash) ___was washing___ her hair when the lights went out.

1. We (play) _____ basketball when it started to rain.

2. I (drive) _____ my car when I crashed into a tree.

3. They (jog) _____ in the park when the snow began.

4. Marvin cut himself while he (shave) _____ this morning.

5. A thief stole our car while we (read) _____ in the library.

6. She fell on the sidewalk while she (ride) _____ her bicycle.

7. I got paint all over myself while I (sit) _____ on a bench in the park.

B. Fill in the blanks.

Ex. I enjoyed ___myself___ at the museum.

1. We didn't enjoy _____ at the concert.

2. Richard burned _____ while he was cooking on the barbecue.

3. Did you and your husband enjoy _____ at the party?

4. Did you fix the VCR by _____, or did your wife help you?

5. Mr. and Mrs. Lopez cut _____ while they were fixing their fence.

6. Nobody went skating with Kate. She had to go skating by _____.

C. Circle the correct answers.

1. When I saw Jill, she was getting | off / of / in | a bus.

2. I usually get | at / up / on | the subway at First Street.

3. When the teacher walked | out of / off / of | the room, everybody started to talk.

4. We run | through / off / on | the park every day.

5. They were walking | from / into / at | the bank when I saw them.

6. The mail carrier | could / couldn't / can't | deliver our mail yesterday because our dog bit him.

7. I'm sorry you | couldn't / were able to / won't be able to | go to the baseball game with us tomorrow.

(continued)

8. When I was a teenager, I wanted to go out with my friends every night, but I

| could
couldn't
had to | because I | could
couldn't
had to | study. |

D. Fill in the blanks.

1. Bill _____ able to go to the beach yesterday because it was raining.

2. I'm glad you _____ able to help me with my science project next weekend.

3. Sally and Jane _____ able to walk home from the party because it was too dark.

4. I couldn't pay my rent last month, but

   I'm sure _____ able to pay it next month.

5. I'm sorry I _____ able to arrive on time yesterday afternoon.

   I _____ fix a flat tire.

6. If you want to put your hair in a ponytail,

   _____ got to have long hair.

7. My daughter _____ able to go to school next week because

   _____ got to have an operation.

E. Listen to the story, and then choose the correct answers to the questions you hear.

Poor Janet!

1. a. She could dance in the school play.
   b. She wasn't able to dance in the school play.

2. a. She practiced every day.
   b. She didn't practice.

3. a. She fell down and cut herself.
   b. She fell down and hurt herself.

4. a. She'll be able to dance in the play.
   b. She can't dance in the play this year.

A MATCHING

You're going for a checkup tomorrow. What will happen?

<u>d</u> 1. The nurse will lead you   **a.** a chest X-ray.

_____ 2. You'll stand   **b.** your heart with a stethoscope.

_____ 3. The nurse will measure   **c.** about your health.

_____ 4. A lab technician will do   **d.** into an examination room.

_____ 5. An X-ray technician will take   **e.** your height and weight.

_____ 6. The doctor will listen to   **f.** a cardiogram.

_____ 7. The doctor will do   **g.** on a scale.

_____ 8. The doctor will talk to you   **h.** some blood tests.

B HOW WAS YOUR MEDICAL CHECKUP?

1. I had a complete _____.
    a. health
    (b.) examination

2. First, the nurse led me into _____.
    a. a test
    b. an examination room

3. I _____ on a scale.
    a. stood
    b. examined

4. The nurse measured my _____.
    a. heart
    b. height

5. Then she _____ my blood pressure.
    a. took
    b. did

6. The lab technician did some _____.
    a. blood tests
    b. blood pressure

7. The doctor _____ my hand.
    a. look
    b. shook

8. He _____ my throat.
    a. listened
    b. examined

9. He did a _____.
    a. cardiogram
    b. stethoscope

10. He talked with me about my _____.
    a. healthy
    b. health

C WENDY IS WORRIED ABOUT HER HEALTH

less	fewer	more

Wendy is worried about her health. She always feels tired, and she doesn't know why. In January, Wendy went to see Dr. Jansen. Dr. Jansen thinks Wendy feels tired because she eats too much sugar. According to Dr. Jansen, Wendy must eat (–) __fewer__ ¹ cookies and (–) _____ ² ice cream.

Also, Wendy must eat (+) _____ ³ green vegetables and (+) _____ ⁴ nuts. Wendy tried Dr. Jansen's diet, but it didn't help.

In March, Wendy went to see Dr. Martin. Dr. Martin thinks Wendy feels tired because she's too thin. According to Dr. Martin, Wendy must eat (–) _____ ⁵ vegetables and (–) _____ ⁶ lean meat. Also, Wendy must eat (+) _____ ⁷ candy and (+) _____ ⁸ potatoes. Wendy tried Dr. Martin's diet, but it didn't help.

In April, Wendy went to see Dr. Appleton. Dr. Appleton thinks Wendy feels tired because she eats too much spicy food. According to Dr. Appleton, Wendy must eat (–) _____ ⁹ pepper and (–) _____ ¹⁰ onions. Also, Wendy must drink (+) _____ ¹¹ skim milk and (+) _____ ¹² water. Wendy tried Dr. Appleton's diet, but it didn't help.

In May, Wendy went to see Dr. Mayfield. Dr. Mayfield thinks Wendy feels tired because she eats too much salt. According to Dr. Mayfield, Wendy must eat (–) _____ ¹³ french fries and (–) _____ ¹⁴ salt. Also, Wendy must eat (+) _____ ¹⁵ yogurt and (+) _____ ¹⁶ fish. Wendy tried Dr. Mayfield's diet, but it didn't help.

Now Wendy needs YOUR help. What do you think?

Wendy must eat/drink (–) _____

_____

Also, she must eat/drink (+) _____

_____

Candy,   cookies,   ice cream, cake!

Candy,   cookies,   ice cream, cake!

Eat less   candy!

Fewer   cookies!

Eat less   ice cream!

Eat less   cake!

Candy,   cookies,   ice cream, cake!

Candy,   cookies,   ice cream, cake!

Carrots,   beans,   grapefruit, greens!

Carrots,   beans,   grapefruit, greens!

Eat more   carrots!

Eat more   beans!

Eat more   grapefruit!

Eat more   greens!

Carrots,   beans,   grapefruit, greens!

Carrots,   beans,   grapefruit, greens!

must		answer	dress	repair	type

1. Here at the Greenly Company, you

   ___must dress___ neatly, and

   you ___must type___ accurately.

2. Remember, you _____ the

   telephone politely, and you _____

   _____ the cars carefully.

must		arrive	file	sort	work

3. Here at the Tip Top Company, every

   employee _____ on time

   and _____ hard.

4. It's very important. You _____

   the mail carefully, and you _____

   _____ accurately.

must		cook	dance	sing	speak

5. Remember, Ginger, you _____

   gracefully, and you _____

   beautifully.

6. Here at Joe's Diner, you _____

   the food quickly, and you _____

   _____ to the customers politely.

WHAT'S THE WORD?

mustn't	don't have to	doesn't have to

1. You _____ mustn't _____ arrive late for work.

2. Helen's doctor is concerned. He says she _____ eat too much candy.

3. According to my doctor, I _____ stop jogging, but I _____ jog so often.

4. Tomorrow is a holiday. The store is closed. The employees _____ work.

5. It's early. You _____ leave right now. But remember, you _____ leave too late.

6. My landlord is upset. He says I _____ play music after midnight.

7. Charlie is lucky. He _____ call the plumber because he was able to fix the sink by himself.

G **THE BUTLER SCHOOL**

must	mustn't	don't have to

At the Butler School you _____ must _____[1] get to school on time

every morning. If you're late, your parents _____[2] write a note.

If you're sick, your parents _____[3] call the school.

You can bring your lunch if you want to, but you

_____[4] because we have a very nice cafeteria.

The boys _____[5] always wear jackets, but if they don't want to wear ties, they

_____[6]. The girls _____[7] wear dresses or skirts. Some girls want to wear

pants to school, but at the Butler School they _____[8]. Everyone _____[9]

have a notebook for every subject, and you _____[10] forget to take your notebooks to

class. You can talk to your friends while you're working, but you _____[11] talk too

loudly. You _____[12] speak politely to your teacher, but you _____[13] agree

with your teacher all the time. If you have a different opinion, your teacher will be happy to

listen. Finally, you _____[14] always do your homework.

H WRITE ABOUT YOUR SCHOOL

At our school, you must ....

You mustn't ....

You don't have to ....

I YOU DECIDE: *What Did They Say?*

must	mustn't

1. My parents told me ....

.... because I have a big test tomorrow.

2. Sally talked to her English teacher, and he told her ....

.... because she makes too many mistakes.

3. Robert talked to his girlfriend and she told him ....

.... because he works too much.

4. Grandpa talked to his doctor and she told him ....

.... because he's a little too heavy.

5. We talked to our landlord and he told us ....

.... because the neighbors are upset.

6. I talked to my grandmother and she told me ....

.... because life is short.

J LISTENING

Listen and choose the correct answer.

1. a. You should watch TV more often.
   b. You must stop watching TV so often.

2. a. You must lose some weight.
   b. You should start eating rich desserts.

3. a. I should stop eating spicy foods.
   b. I must start eating spicy foods.

4. a. You must stop relaxing.
   b. You must take life a little easier.

5. a. You must start listening to loud music.
   b. You should stop listening to loud music.

6. a. I must stop jogging.
   b. I should jog more often.

K GRAMMARRAP: *You Mustn't Eat Cookies*

Listen. Then clap and practice.

A. You mustn't eat   cookies.

B. You mustn't eat   cake.

C. You mustn't eat   butter.

D. You mustn't eat   steak.

A. You must eat   fruit.

B. You must eat   potatoes.

C. You must eat   fish.

D. You must eat   tomatoes.

L GRAMMARRAP: *You Must . . .*

Listen. Then clap and practice.

A. You must clean your   room.

B. But I cleaned it on   Sunday!

A. You must do the   laundry.

B. But I did it last   Monday!

A. You must fix the   fence.

B. But I fixed it in   June!

A. You must do your   homework!

B. I'll finish it   soon!

LOUD AND CLEAR h!

Fill in the words. Then read the sentences aloud.

hotel	Hawaii	happy	here
	Hi	Honolulu	

history	Howard	half	hand
	have	homework	

1. ___Hi___! We're ___happy___ we're ___here___ in our ___hotel___ in ___Honolulu___, ___Hawaii___!

2. Hurry, _____! You _____ to _____ in your _____ _____ in _____ an hour.

hurt	Harry	helmet	his
	head	have	

hot dogs	Henry	has	heavy
	height	having	

3. Poor _____! He _____ _____ _____ because he didn't _____ a _____.

4. _____ is too _____ for his _____. He _____ to stop _____ _____.

husband	has	healthy	he
	heart	Hilda's	

hiccups	Hillary	headache	
horrible	happy	has	

5. _____ _____ isn't _____. _____ _____ problems with his hearing and his _____.

6. _____ isn't _____. She _____ the _____ and a _____ _____.

12

| bathe | exercise | iron | knit | mop | pay | rearrange | sew |

1. Will Michael be busy this morning?

___Yes, he will___. ___He'll be mopping___ his floors.

2. Will your children be busy this afternoon?

_____. _____ the dog.

3. Will you and George be busy today?

_____. _____ at the health club.

4. Will Mr. and Mrs. Benson be busy today?

_____. _____ bills.

5. Will Kate be busy tomorrow afternoon?

_____. _____ a sweater.

6. Will you be busy this afternoon?

_____. _____ clothes.

7. Will Fred be busy this Saturday?

_____. _____ shirts.

8. Will you and your wife be busy tomorrow?

_____. _____ furniture.

Arthur was upset after he talked to Gloria. He decided to call Jennifer.

Hi, Jennifer. This is Arthur. Can I come over this afternoon?

No, Arthur. I'm afraid I won't be home this afternoon.

I'll be _____ .

I see. Can I come over TOMORROW afternoon?

No, Arthur. I'm afraid I won't be home tomorrow afternoon.

I'll be _____ .

Can I come over and visit this WEEKEND?

No, Arthur. I'll be _____ .

Well, can I come over and visit next Monday?

No, Arthur. I'll be _____ .

How about some time next AUTUMN?

No, Arthur. I'm getting married next autumn.

Oh, no! Not again!!

GrammarRap: *What Do You Think?*

Listen. Then clap and practice.

A. What do you   think you'll be   doing next   spring?

B. I'll probably be   doing the   same old   thing.

A. What do you   think he'll be   doing this   fall?

B. I'm sure he'll be   working   downtown at the   mall.

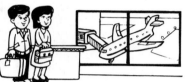

A. When do you   think they'll be   leaving for   Spain?

B. I think they'll be   taking the   four o'clock   plane.

A. When do you   think you'll be   hearing from   Anne?

B. I'm sure she'll be   calling as   soon as she   can.

A. When do you   think we'll be   hearing from   Jack?

B. I'm sure he'll be   phoning as   soon as he's   back.

A. What do you   think she'll be   doing at   two?

B. I think she'll be   taking the   kids to the   zoo.

A. Where do you   think they'll be   living next   year?

B. As far as we   know, they'll be   living right   here.

WHY DON'T YOU?

bake	clean his apartment	exercise	study	wash her car
bathe their dog	do their laundry	practice the violin	take a bath	watch TV

1. A. Why don't you call Jane this Saturday?
    B. I don't want to disturb her. I'm sure

    _____she'll be practicing the violin_____.

    She always _____practices the violin_____
    on Saturday.

2. A. Why don't you call Carlos after dinner?
    B. I don't want to disturb him. I'm sure

    _____.

    He always _____
    after dinner.

3. A. Why don't you call Peggy and Bob
        tonight?
    B. I don't want to disturb them. I'm sure

    _____.

    They always _____
    on Monday night.

4. A. Why don't you call Nancy
        this afternoon?
    B. I don't want to disturb her. I'm sure

    _____.

    She usually _____
    in the afternoon.

5. A. Why don't you call your cousin Henry
        this morning?
    B. I don't want to disturb him. I'm sure

    _____.

    He always _____
    on Sunday morning.

6. A. Why don't you call Tom and Carol
        this evening?
    B. I don't want to disturb them. I'm sure

    _____.

    They always _____
    in the evening.

7. A. Why don't you call Elizabeth this this afternoon?
    B. I don't want to disturb her. I'm sure

    _____.

    She usually _____ on Sunday afternoon.

8. A. Why don't you call your aunt and uncle this morning?
    B. I don't want to disturb them. I'm sure

    _____.

    They always _____ on Saturday morning.

9. A. Why don't you call your friend George tonight?
    B. I don't want to disturb him. I'm sure

    _____.

    He always _____ before he goes to bed.

10. A. Why don't you call Betty and Ben tonight?
    B. I don't want to disturb them. I'm sure

    _____.

    They always _____ on Tuesday night.

 **LISTENING**

Listen and choose the correct answer.

1. a. buying dresses
    b. ironing dresses

2. a. working downtown
    b. walking downtown

3. a. sitting on the front porch
    b. knitting on the front porch

4. a. watching sports
    b. washing shorts

5. a. feeding the baby
    b. reading to the baby

6. a. taking a bus
    b. taking a bath

7. a. making pancakes
    b. baking cakes

8. a. doing her homework
    b. doing yoga

9. a. skiing
    b. sleeping

10. a. skateboarding
    b. skating

11. a. washing the dog
    b. walking the dog

12. a. singing about you
    b. thinking about you

F WHAT'S THE WORD?

called	isn't	message	right	take	that
hello	may	okay	speak	tell	this

A. _____Hello___ ¹.

B. Hello. _____ ² is Brian. _____ ³ I please

_____ ⁴ to Cathy?

A. I'm sorry. Cathy _____ ⁵ here _____ ⁶ now.

Can I _____ ⁷ a _____ ⁸?

B. Yes. Please _____ ⁹ Cathy _____ ¹⁰

Brian _____ ¹¹.

A. _____ ¹².

B. Thank you.

G WHAT'S THE RESPONSE?

Choose the correct response.

1. May I please speak to Ronald?
   a. Thank you.
   b. Yes. Hold on a moment.

2. When can you come over?
   a. At three this afternoon.
   b. Don't worry.

3. I don't want to disturb you.
   a. Yes, I will.
   b. Don't worry. You won't disturb me.

4. We won't be able to come over and visit you tomorrow night.
   a. Oh. Why not?
   b. When?

5. I can come over tonight. Is that okay?
   a. I'll be glad.
   b. Sure. I'll see you then.

6. Sorry. I'll be eating dinner at seven.
   a. I don't want to disturb you.
   b. I'll disturb you.

7. Hello.
   a. Okay.
   b. Hello. This is Mrs. Miller.

8. Hi, Barbara. What's up?
   a. Fine.
   b. I'm having a test tomorrow.

9. I'm afraid I won't be home at three.
   a. Okay. I'll see you at three.
   b. Oh. How about six?

10. I'm having some problems with the homework for tomorrow.
    a. I'll be glad to help.
    b. I'm glad.

11. Will you be home this Wednesday afternoon?
    a. Yes. I'll be shopping.
    b. Yes. I'll be ironing.

12. How about nine o'clock?
    a. Fine. I'll see you then.
    b. Yes, it will.

H UNTIL WHEN?

at	for	in	until

1. A. How much longer will you be practicing the piano?

   B. ____I'll *be practicing*____ the piano ____for____ another half hour.

2. A. How long will Grandpa be reading the newspaper?

   B. _____ the newspaper _____ he falls asleep.

3. A. How late will Jane be working at the office this evening?

   B. _____ at the office _____ ten o'clock.

4. A. Excuse me. When will we be arriving in San Francisco?

   B. _____ in San Francisco _____ six thirty.

5. A. When will you be having your yearly checkup?

   B. _____ my yearly checkup_____ a few weeks.

6. A. How late will Maria be studying English?

   B. _____ English _____ 8:30.

7. A. How long will your Uncle Willy be staying with us?

   B. _____ with us _____ next month.

8. A. How much longer will you be cooking on the barbecue?

   B. _____ on the barbecue _____ another ten minutes.

Activity Workbook   117

1. How much longer _will you be talking on the telephone_ ?

I'll be talking on the telephone for another half hour.

2. A. How late _____ ?

   B. They'll be arriving at midnight.

3. A. How long _____ ?

   B. She'll be working on his car all morning.

4. A. When _____ ?

   B. He'll be leaving in a little while.

5. A. How far _____ ?

   B. We'll be driving until we get to Miami.

6. A. How long _____ ?

   B. I'll be mopping the floors all morning.

7. A. How soon _____ ?

   B. She'll be feeding the dog when she gets home.

8. A. How much longer _____ ?

   B. They'll be living away from home until they finish college.

9. A. How late _____ ?

   B. He'll be playing loud music until 2 A.M.

10. How much longer _____ ?

We'll be riding on the roller-coaster for another five minutes.

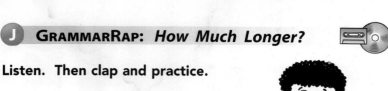

Listen. Then clap and practice.

A. How much   longer will you be   talking on the   phone?

B. I'll be talking for a   few more   minutes.

A. For a few more   minutes?

B. That's what I   said.

  I'll be talking for a   few more   minutes.

A. How much   longer will he be   working   at the mall?

B. He'll be working for a   few more   hours.

A. For a few more   hours?

B. That's what he   said.

  He'll be working for a   few more   hours.

A. How much   longer will she be staying in   Rome?

B. She'll be staying for a   few more   days.

A. For a few more   days?

B. That's what she   said.

  She'll be staying for a   few more   days.

13

me	him	her	us	you	them
my	his	her	our	your	their
myself	himself	herself	ourselves	yourself	themselves
				yourselves	

1. _____His_____ family didn't help

_____him_____. He painted the fence

by _____himself_____.

2. _____ parents didn't help

_____. They made breakfast

by _____.

3. _____ mother usually helps

_____ put her hair in a ponytail.

But today she did it by _____.

4. Do you need any help? I'll help _____.

_____ don't have to rake the leaves

by _____.

5. Nobody is helping _____.

He's washing the dishes by _____.

6. I planted these flowers by _____.

Nobody helped _____.

7. _____ teacher can't help

_____. We've got to do our

homework by _____.

8. You don't have to go on the roller coaster

by _____. I'll go with

_____.

B THE LOST ROLLERBLADES

mine	his	hers	ours	yours	theirs

A. I just found these rollerblades. Are they ____yours____ [1]?

B. No. They aren't _____ [2]. But they might be Jim's. He always forgets things.

A. No. I don't think they're _____ [3]. His rollerblades are green, and these are black.

B. Do you think they might be Ms. Johnson's?

A. Our English teacher's?! No. They can't be _____ [4]. She doesn't have rollerblades.

B. How about Carol and Ted? Do you think these rollerblades might

be _____ [5]?

A. No, I don't think so. They never go rollerblading. I have an idea. Let's put the rollerblades in the school office.

B. Okay. And if nobody asks for them soon, I guess they'll be _____ [6].

C SCRAMBLED SENTENCES

Unscramble the sentences.

1. his   he   by   fix   himself?   Did   car

   _____ Did he fix his car by himself? _____

2. book   Is   yours?   address   this

   _____

3. cats   feed   by   She   can   the   herself.

   _____

4. you   number?   Did   her   him   telephone   give

   _____

5. Bob,   I   new   When   him   you   tell   call   his   sunglasses.   have

   _____

6. lost   because   to   cell   your   I   mine.   need   use   phone   I

   _____

Choose the correct word.

1. I like to eat the _____ stew.
   a. chef's
   b. chefs'

2. I love my _____ birthday presents!
   a. grandmother's
   b. grandmothers'

3. Where's the _____ food?
   a. cat's
   b. cats'

4. Do you listen to your _____ CDs?
   a. sons'
   b. son's

5. These are probably a _____ headphones.
   a. student's
   b. students'

6. Is this your _____ ring?
   a. girlfriends'
   b. girlfriend's

7. My _____ new painting is very ugly.
   a. cousin's
   b. cousins'

8. My _____ dog usually barks all night.
   a. neighbor's
   b. neighbors'

Listen to each conversation, and then choose the correct answers to the questions you hear.

CONVERSATION 1

1. a. On the floor.
   b. On the desk.
   c. On the chair.

2. a. No, it isn't his.
   b. It might be his.
   c. Yes, it's his.

3. a. Last Tuesday.
   b. Last Monday.
   c. Last Thursday.

CONVERSATION 2

4. a. Black.
   b. Brown.
   c. Blue.

5. a. Her watch.
   b. Her umbrella.
   c. Her wallet.

6. a. Yes, it's hers.
   b. No, it isn't hers.
   c. It might be hers.

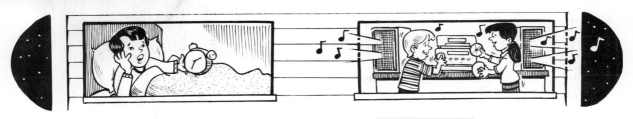

It's 1:30 A.M., and James can't fall asleep because his [neighbors / (neighbors')]¹ children

[are listening / will be listening]² to loud music. Last night they [listened / listening]³ to loud music [until / for]⁴

four hours, and James [couldn't / wasn't]⁵ able to [fall / fell]⁶ asleep. He's very worried because he

studies [hardly / hard]⁷ every day, and he needs to sleep [at / in the]⁸ night. Tomorrow he thinks

[he'll call / he calls]⁹ [him / his]¹⁰ landlord.

It's 2 A.M., and I'm not asleep because my [next-door / downstairs]¹¹ neighbors are rearranging

[there / their]¹² furniture. They're very [noisily / noisy]¹³! I don't like [complain / to complain]¹⁴, but if they

[move / will move]¹⁵ furniture again tomorrow night, I'll talk [to / at]¹⁶ the landlord, or I'll call them

[themselves / myself]¹⁷.

(continued)

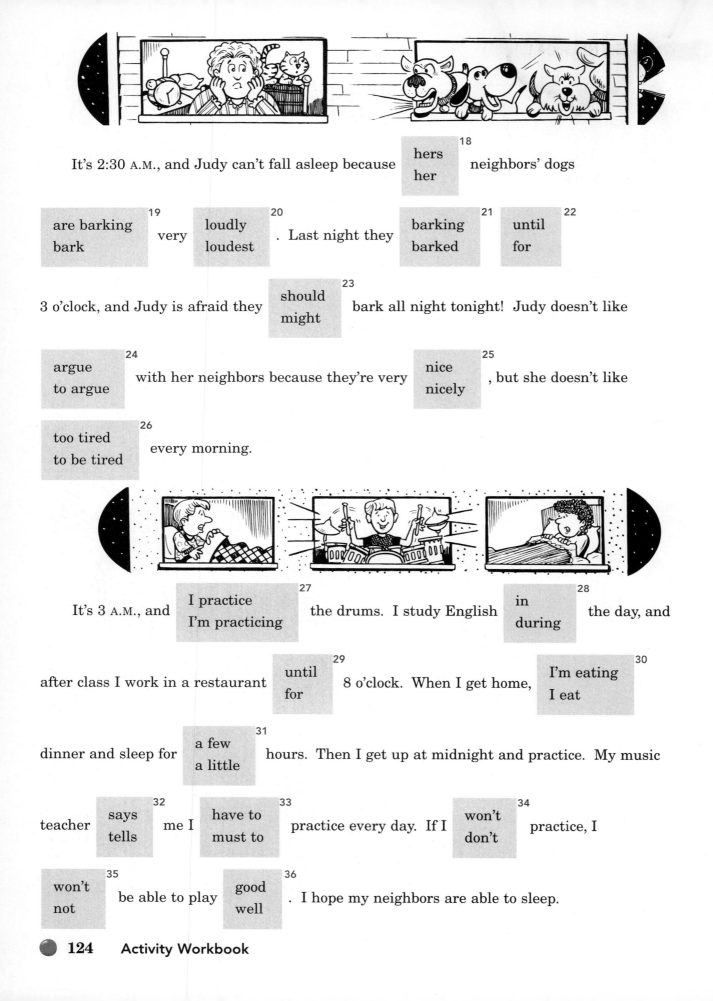

It's 2:30 A.M., and Judy can't fall asleep because [hers / her]¹⁸ neighbors' dogs

[are barking / bark]¹⁹ very [loudly / loudest]²⁰. Last night they [barking / barked]²¹ [until / for]²²

3 o'clock, and Judy is afraid they [should / might]²³ bark all night tonight! Judy doesn't like

[argue / to argue]²⁴ with her neighbors because they're very [nice / nicely]²⁵, but she doesn't like

[too tired / to be tired]²⁶ every morning.

It's 3 A.M., and [I practice / I'm practicing]²⁷ the drums. I study English [in / during]²⁸ the day, and

after class I work in a restaurant [until / for]²⁹ 8 o'clock. When I get home, [I'm eating / I eat]³⁰

dinner and sleep for [a few / a little]³¹ hours. Then I get up at midnight and practice. My music

teacher [says / tells]³² me I [have to / must to]³³ practice every day. If I [won't / don't]³⁴ practice, I

[won't / not]³⁵ be able to play [good / well]³⁶. I hope my neighbors are able to sleep.

1. A. I don't like Stuart. He never says [anyone / (anything)] nice.

   B. To tell the truth, [nobody / anybody] likes Stuart. He never

   says [anything / something] nice about [nobody / anybody] !

2. A. I can't fix my video camera. Is there [anyone / anything] you can do to help?

   B. No. I'm afraid [nobody / somebody] here can help you.

   You'll have to fix it by [himself / yourself] .

3. A. Look! [Anybody / Somebody] ate all the cake!

   B. That's terrible! [Anybody / Nobody] will be able to

   have it for dessert tonight!

4. A. There's [anyone / someone] on the phone for you.

   B. Who is it?

   A. I don't have [any / some] idea.

(continued)

5. A. I can't hook up my new printer. Does [anybody / nobody] here know how to do it?

B. You should ask the supervisor. She knows [anyone / someone] who can do it.

6. A. How was the party last night?

B. It was terrible! I didn't know [anyone / somebody] there,

and [anybody / nobody] talked to me.

7. A. What's that noise? I think [anybody / somebody] is in the basement!

B. I don't hear [nothing / anything]. Don't worry. [Nobody / Anybody] is in the basement.

A. Are you sure? I definitely hear [anything / something].

B. Don't worry. [Nobody / Anybody] is there.

H **LISTENING:** *The Prom*

Listen and choose the correct response.

1. a. No, I wasn't.
    (b.) I didn't enjoy myself very much.

2. a. It wasn't very comfortable.
    b. She was very talkative.

3. a. It was too crowded.
    b. It was too soft.

4. a. Until 10:30.
    b. In a few hours.

5. a. I missed the bus.
    b. I wasn't having a good time.

6. a. I'm sure it is.
    b. We'll just have to wait and see.

A. Hello. May I please speak to Maggie Winters?

B. ....

A. There's something wrong with my dishwasher, and I need a repairperson who can come over and fix it.

B. ....

A. No. There isn't any water on the kitchen floor, but the dishwasher won't turn on.

B. ....

A. I don't know. It worked yesterday, but it isn't working today.

B. ....

A. I live at 234 School Street in Westville.

B. ....

A. Drive down Center Street and turn right. My house is the last one on the left.

B. ....

A. I'm sorry. I'm afraid I won't be home at 9:00 tomorrow morning. Can you come at any other time?

B. ....

A. Can you come a little earlier?

B. ....

A. That's fine. I'll see you then. Good-bye.

B. Good-bye.

J **GrammarRap:** *I Clean It Myself*

Listen. Then clap and practice.

A.　　　Who cleans your　house?

B.　　　I clean it　　　myself.

A. Does your wife　　　help you?

B.　　　She helps me if I　ask her.

A.　　　Who washes the　dishes?

B.　　　He washes them himself.

A. Does his daughter　　help him?

B.　　　She helps him if he　asks her.

A.　　　Who does your　shopping?

B.　　　We do it　　　ourselves.

A. Do your children　　help you?

B.　　　They help us if we　ask them.

A.　　　Who does your　laundry?

B.　　　I do it　　　myself.

A. Does your husband　help you?

B.　　　He helps me if I　ask him.

A.　　　Who makes　breakfast?

B.　　　She makes it　herself.

A. Does her father　　help her?

B.　　　He helps her if she　asks him.

A.　　　Who does their　homework?

B.　　　They do it　　themselves.

A. Does their mother　　help them?

B.　　　She helps them if they ask her.

K YOU DECIDE: *Why Can't They Go to the Baseball Game?*

A. Would you like to go to a baseball game with me on Saturday?

B. ....

A. That's too bad. Do you think your sister might be able to go?

B. ....

A. Oh, I forgot. She's busy every Saturday. How about your cousins? They like baseball.

B. ....

A. Oh. I hope they enjoy themselves. Do you think your father might want to go?

B. ....

A. That's too bad. Nobody told me. How did it happen?

B. ....

A. Well, I hope he's better soon. You know, I guess I'll go to work on Saturday.

B. ....

A. Really? Our boss likes baseball?!

B. ....

A. Okay. I'll call him and see if he wants to go with me. Good-bye.

B. ....

L LISTENING

Listen and choose the person you should call.

1. a. a plumber
   b. a mechanic
   c. a doctor

2. a. a lab technician
   b. an electrician
   c. a plumber

3. a. a doctor
   b. a locksmith
   c. a dentist

4. a. a mechanic
   b. a plumber
   c. the landlord

5. a. an electrician
   b. a plumber
   c. a painter

6. a. a mechanic
   b. the police
   c. a repairperson

7. a. a chef
   b. an electrician
   c. a plumber

8. a. a teacher
   b. a repairperson
   c. a mechanic

(In item 1, answer **b.** is circled.)

M WHAT'S THE WORD?

Circle the correct word.

1. Too / **Two** cats are too / two many cats for me!

2. Last weak / week I was too weak / week to get out of bed.

3. Their / They're going to go for their / they're annual physical examination.

4. You're right / write . I should right / write my term paper this weekend.

5. Wear / Where are my glasses? I need to wear / where them.

6. We have an our / hour to do our / hour exercises.

7. Do you no / know a good dentist? No, / Know, I don't.

8. You should by / buy a camera and take pictures of your children by / buy yourself.

9. There's a big hole / whole in my slice of hole / whole wheat bread!

10. You're / Your late. You're / Your guests arrived twenty minutes ago.

11. Yesterday they cooked ate / eight cakes for a party, and the guests ate / eight all the cakes.

Listen. Then clap and practice.

Does anybody   here speak   Spanish?

Does anybody   here speak   French?

Does anybody   here have a   hammer?

Does anyone   here have a   wrench?

Somebody   here speaks   Spanish.

Somebody   here speaks   French.

Somebody   here has a   hammer.

Someone   here has a   wrench.

Does anybody   here have   change for a   dollar?

Does anyone   here have   a dime?

Does anybody   here have a   map of the   city?

Does anyone   here have the   time?

Nobody   here has   change for a   dollar.

Nobody   here has   a dime.

Nobody   here has a   map of the   city.

Nobody   here has the   time.

A. Complete the sentences.

Ex. Will you be home this evening?
Yes, I will. (knit)

_____ I'll *be knitting* _____ .

1. Will your parents be busy today?
Yes, they will. (pay)

_____ bills.

2. Will you be leaving home soon?
Yes, I will. (go)

_____ to college.

3. Will your brother be home at 5:00?
Yes, he will. (read)

_____ his e-mail.

4. Will Karen be at the office tonight?
Yes, she will. (work)

_____ until 9:00.

5. Will you and your girlfriend be busy
this Saturday?
Yes, we will. (get married)

_____ .

B. Complete the sentences.

Ex. When _____ will you be visiting us _____?
We'll be visiting you next January.

1. How late _____

_____?
I'll be practicing the piano until 8:00.

2. How much longer _____

_____?
He'll be ironing for a few more
minutes.

3. How soon _____

_____?
She'll be leaving in a little while.

4. How far _____

_____?
They'll be driving until they get to Denver.

5. How long _____

_____?
We'll be chatting online for a few hours.

C. Circle the correct answers.

1. My doctor says I must eat [less / fewer] ice cream, [less / fewer] french fries, and [less / fewer] fatty meat.

2. I [mustn't / don't have to] solve this math problem tonight, but I want to.

3. Jim [mustn't / doesn't have to] eat too [much / many] spicy food because he has stomach problems.

4. If you want to get a job in this office, you must speak English and Spanish, but you [mustn't / don't have to] type very fast.

5. My son will be performing in the school play [for / until] a week.

6. She'll be staying in Chicago [for / until] Friday.

7. They finished [at / in] 8:00.

8. I'll be arriving [at / in] noon.

9. I need [anyone / someone] who can fix my

camcorder. I don't know [anything / something]

about camcorders.

10. If you look in the phone book, I'm sure you'll

find [anybody / somebody] who can fix your VCR.

11. [Anyone / Someone] borrowed my mop, and now

I can't clean the floors.

12. This is his car. It isn't [my / mine].

13. I don't think this is [their / theirs] cell phone,

but it might be [her / hers].

14. We gave [her / his] our headphones.

15. This camera isn't [ours / our].

D. **Listen and choose the correct answers to complete the sentences.**

1. a. a complete physical examination.
   b. an examination room.

2. a. your blood.
   b. your height and your weight.

3. a. blood pressure.
   b. stethoscope.

4. a. a pulse.
   b. an X-ray.

5. a. eyes, ears, nose, and throat.
   b. checkup.

APPENDIX

Listening Scripts

Page 2 Exercise B

Listen and choose the correct response.

1. What do your friends like to do on the weekend?
2. What does your sister like to do on the weekend?
3. What does your brother like to do on the weekend?
4. What do you and your friends like to do on the weekend?
5. What does your son like to do on the weekend?
6. What do you like to do on the weekend?
7. What does your next-door neighbor like to do on the weekend?
8. What does your cousin Sue like to do on the weekend?

Page 10 Exercise N

Listen and write the ordinal number you hear.

Many people live and work in this large apartment building in New York City.

1. There's a barber shop on the second floor.
2. The Wong family lives on the twelfth floor.
3. The Acme Internet Company is on the thirtieth floor.
4. Bob Richards lives on the thirteenth floor.
5. There's a bank on the third floor.
6. There's a dentist's office on the ninth floor.
7. There's a flower shop on the first floor.
8. The Martinez family lives on the nineteenth floor.
9. Louise Lane works on the seventeenth floor.
10. There's a computer store on the fourth floor.
11. There's an expensive French restaurant on the forty-eighth floor.
12. My apartment is on the fifth floor.
13. The Park family lives on the thirty-fourth floor.
14. Dr. Jacobson has an office on the twenty-sixth floor.
15. The Walker family lives on the sixty-second floor.
16. There's a health club on the eighteenth floor.

Page 13 Exercise C

Listen and choose the correct response.

1. Where's the tea?
2. Where are the oranges?
3. Where's the fish?
4. Where are the cookies?
5. Where's the cake?
6. Where's the rice?
7. Where are the pears?
8. Where's the cheese?

Page 15 Exercise F

Listen and put a check under the correct picture.

1. Let's have some pizza!
2. Where are the eggs?
3. Let's make some fresh orange juice!
4. Let's bake a pie!
5. Where are the potatoes?
6. Let's have a sandwich for lunch!

Page 19 Exercise L

Listen and put a check under the correct picture.

1. A. Would you care for some more?
   B. Yes, please. But not too much.
2. A. Do you like them?
   B. Yes, but my doctor says that too many are bad for my health.
3. A. These are wonderful!
   B. I'm glad you like them. I bought them this morning.
4. A. How much did you eat?
   B. I ate too much!
5. A. I bought it this morning, and it's very good. Would you like a little?
   B. Yes, please.
6. A. I really don't like them.
   B. But they're good for you!
7. A. How do you like them?
   B. They're wonderful.
8. A. Would you care for some more?
   B. Yes, please. But not too much.
9. A. Hmm. This is delicious. Would you care for some more?
   B. Yes, please. But just a little.
10. A. This is delicious!
    B. I'm glad you like it. I made it this morning.

Page 22 Exercise C

Listen to the conversations. Put a check under the foods you hear.

1. A. Do we need anything from the supermarket?
   B. Yes. We need a pound of apples, a bunch of bananas, and a head of lettuce.
2. A. What do we need at the supermarket?
   B. We need a pound of cheese, a box of rice, and a bottle of soda.
3. A. Do we need anything from the supermarket?
   B. Yes. We need a loaf of bread, a pound of onions, and a dozen oranges.
4. A. What do we need at the supermarket?
   B. We need a pound of potatoes, a pint of ice cream, and a jar of mustard.

Page 24 Exercise F

Listen and circle the price you hear.

1. A box of cereal costs a dollar ninety-nine.
2. Two cans cost five dollars.
3. Three jars cost four dollars and seventy-nine cents.
4. It costs twenty-five cents.
5. A bottle costs two forty-seven.
6. Two boxes cost six dollars and sixty cents.
7. Three thirteen?! That's a lot of money!
8. A pound costs a dollar fifty.
9. Two dollars and ten cents?! That's cheap!

Page 27 Exercise M

Listen and choose the correct word to complete the sentence.

1. Add a little . . .
2. Chop up a few . . .
3. Cut up a few . . .
4. Pour in a little . . .
5. Slice a few . . .
6. Mix in a little . . .

Page 29 Exercise E

Listen and circle the correct word.

Ex. I want some lemons.
1. I'd like some ice cream.
2. I need some tomatoes.
3. I'm looking for lettuce.
4. May I have some meatballs?
5. I want some whole wheat bread.

Page 32 Exercise D

Listen and circle the words you hear.

1. I want to have the chocolate ice cream.
2. They won't fax the letter this morning.
3. I want to recommend the fish today.
4. Peter and William won't go home this morning.
5. She won't eat meat.
6. They want to get married soon.
7. He won't buy a car this year.
8. We want to use our computer now.

Page 37 Exercise K

Listen and choose the correct answer.

1. I'm afraid I might get sick!
2. I'm afraid I might fall asleep!
3. I'm afraid I might step on your feet!
4. I'm afraid I might break my leg!
5. I'm afraid I might catch a cold!
6. I'm afraid I might drown.
7. I'm afraid I might get seasick!
8. I'm afraid I might get a sunburn!
9. I'm afraid I might have a terrible time!
10. I'm afraid I might look terrible!

Page 42 Exercise F

Listen and choose the correct words to complete the sentences.

1. A. Yesterday was cool.
   B. I know. But today is . . .
2. A. Ronald is tall.
   B. You're right. But his son Jim is . . .
3. A. This briefcase is very attractive.
   B. Really? I think THAT briefcase is . . .
4. A. Nancy is very nice.
   B. Do you know her sister Sally? She's . . .
5. A. Tom is very fast.
   B. You're right. But his brother John is . . .
6. A. Michael is a very friendly person.
   B. I know. But his wife is . . .
7. A. Your roommate is very interesting.
   B. You're right. But I think YOUR roommate is . . .
8. A. The supermarket on Center Street was very busy today.
   B. Yes, I know. But the supermarket on Main Street was . . .

Page 44 Exercise I

Listen and circle the correct answer.

1. Yesterday was hotter than today.
2. The tomatoes are more expensive than the potatoes.
3. Aunt Betty is younger than cousin Jane.
4. Bob is shorter and heavier than Bill.
5. Barry's chair is more comfortable than Larry's chair.
6. The science test was more difficult than the history test.
7. Irene's office is bigger than Eileen's office.
8. Ronald is more capable than Donald.

Page 56 Exercise F

Listen and circle the words you hear.

1. My new chair is much more comfortable than my old chair.
2. Is that the worst city in the country?
3. I want a more energetic president.
4. Don't you have a cheaper one?
5. What was the most important day in your life?
6. Roger is the sloppiest teenager I know.
7. This is the best perfume we have.
8. Sally isn't as lazy as Richard is.
9. You know, I think your dog is meaner than mine.
10. Howard is the most honest person I know.

Page 59 Exercise G

Listen and circle the correct answer.

Ex. Ronald is younger than Fred.
1. Bob is neater than Bill.
2. The chicken is more expensive than the fish.
3. Moscow is warmer than Miami.
4. Herbert is taller than Steven.
5. Patty is more talented than Pam.

Page 63 Exercise D

Look at the map on page 62. Listen and choose the correct answer.

1. Linda was at the hotel on Ninth Avenue. She walked along Ninth Avenue to Elm Street and turned right. She walked up Elm Street to Eighth Avenue and turned right again. She went to a building on the left, between the flower shop and the post office.

2. Roger was at the shoe store on Eighth Avenue. He walked along Eighth Avenue to Oak Street and turned right. He walked down Oak Street and went to a building on the left, across from the parking garage.

3. Mr. and Mrs. Baker were at the book store on Elm Street. They walked up Elm Street to Eighth Avenue and turned right. They walked along Eighth Avenue to a building next to the pet shop and across from the post office.

4. Wanda was at the department store on Ninth Avenue. She walked along Ninth Avenue to Oak Street and turned left. She walked up Oak Street to a building on the right, next to the toy store and across from the library.

5. Alan was at the motel on Oak Street. He walked down Oak Street to Ninth Avenue and turned right. He walked along Ninth Avenue to a place on the left, next to the supermarket and across from the department store.

6. Alice was at the supermarket on Ninth Avenue. She walked along Ninth Avenue to Oak Street and turned left. She walked up Oak Street to Eighth Avenue and turned right. She went to a building on the left, across from the restaurant.

Page 67 Exercise I

Listen and fill in the correct places.

1. David took the Bay Avenue bus and got off at Second Street. He walked up Second Street to Brighton Boulevard and turned right. He walked along Brighton Boulevard to a building on the right, across from the post office. Where did he go?

2. Barbara took the Day Street bus and got off at Second Street. She walked down Second Street to Bay Avenue and turned right. She walked along Bay Avenue to a building between the flower shop and the church. Where did she go?

3. Mr. and Mrs. Jackson took the Bay Avenue bus and got off at First Street. They walked up First Street to Brighton Boulevard and turned left. They walked along Brighton Boulevard to a building on the right, next to the bus station and across from the barber shop. Where did they go?

4. Susan didn't want to take the bus this morning. She was at the library on Bay Avenue. She walked along Bay Avenue to Third Street and turned left. She walked up Third Street to Day Street and turned left again. She walked along Day Street and went to a building on the left, between First Street and Second Street. Where did she go?

5. Mr. and Mrs. Yamamoto wanted to get some exercise this morning. They took the Day Street bus and got off at First Street. They walked down First Street to Brighton Boulevard and turned left. They walked along Brighton Boulevard to Second Street and turned right. They walked down Second Street to Bay Avenue and turned right again. They went to a place on the right, at the corner of First Street and Bay Avenue, next to the concert hall. Where did they go?

6. George got lost this morning. He took the Bay Avenue bus and got off at First Street. He walked up First Street to Brighton Boulevard and turned right. He walked along Brighton Boulevard to Second Street and turned left. He walked up Second Street to Day Street and turned right. He walked along Day Street to Third Street and turned right again. He walked down Third Street to Brighton Boulevard, and then he was happy. He went to a place at the corner of Third Street and Brighton Boulevard, next to the post office and across from the pet shop. Where did he go?

Page 69 Exercise C

Listen and circle the correct word to complete the sentence.

1. He's a good worker, but he's . . .
2. She's an excellent violinist. She plays the violin . . .
3. I don't think he's an honest card player. To tell the truth, everybody says he's . . .
4. I can't read their homework because they write very . . .

5. Maria never makes mistakes. She's very . . .
6. Their son Marvin is very polite. He never speaks . . .
7. When you leave the party, please drive home . . .
8. Their car is very old. I don't think it's . . .
9. People can't hear you very well when you speak . . .
10. We never buy expensive clothes. We live very . . .
11. You rode your motorcycle carelessly yesterday. That's strange. You usually ride it very . . .
12. Everybody in the store likes Jane. She works hard, and when she talks to customers she's very . . .

Page 80 Exercise F

Listen and fill in the correct places.

1. Mrs. Mendoza was at the hotel at the corner of First Avenue and Grove Street. She walked up Grove Street to Second Avenue and turned left. She walked along Second Avenue to a building on the left, between the pet shop and the cafeteria. Where did she go?

2. Edward was at the football stadium on First Avenue. He walked along First Avenue to Elm Street and turned left. He walked up Elm Street to Second Avenue and turned right. He walked along Second Avenue to a building on the right, at the corner of Grove Street and Second Avenue, across from the bank. Where did he go?

3. Mr. and Mrs. Wong were at the post office on Second Avenue. They walked along Second Avenue to Grove Street and turned left. They walked down Grove Street to First Avenue and turned right. They went to a building on the left, across from the museum and the parking garage. Where did they go?

4. Thomas was at the hospital on Second Avenue. He walked along Second Avenue to Elm Street and turned right. He walked down Elm Street to First Avenue and turned left. He walked along First Avenue to a building on the left, at the corner of Grove Street and First Avenue, across from the supermarket. Where did he go?

5. Maria was at the shoe store on First Avenue. She walked along First Avenue to Grove Street and turned left. She walked up Grove Street to Second Avenue and turned left again. She walked along Second Avenue to a building on the right, between the toy store and the barber shop, across from the ice cream shop. Where did she go?

Page 83 Exercise E

Listen and choose the correct answer.

1. A. What was he doing yesterday when the lights went out?
   B. He was shaving.
2. A. What was she doing yesterday when you saw her?
   B. She was skating.
3. A. What were they doing when it started to rain?
   B. They were swimming at the beach.
4. A. What was he doing yesterday when you called?
   B. He was studying math.
5. A. What were you doing when your friends arrived?
   B. We were eating.
6. A. What was she doing when you saw her?
   B. She was talking with her mother.
7. A. What was he doing when you called?
   B. He was taking a shower.
8. A. What were you doing when the guests arrived?
   B. I was sweeping the living room.

Page 84 Exercise G

Listen and put the number under the correct picture.

1. I saw you yesterday at about 3:00. You were walking into the bank.
2. I saw you yesterday at about 1:30. You were jogging through the park.
3. I saw you yesterday at about 2:00. You were getting off the D Train.
4. I saw you yesterday at about 5:00. You were getting on the B Train.
5. I saw you yesterday at about 4:45. You were getting out of a taxi on Fifth Street.
6. I saw you yesterday at about noon. You were getting into a taxi on Sixth Street.
7. I saw you yesterday at about 11:45. You were getting on a bus.
8. I saw you yesterday at about 9:00. You were getting off a bus.

Page 88 Exercise M

Listen and choose the correct answer.

1. A. Why does Sally look so upset?
   B. She lost her new boot.
2. A. What happened to Howard?
   B. He burned himself while he was cooking.
3. A. When did you see them?
   B. While they were walking out of the park.
4. A. You look upset. What happened?
   B. Someone stole our new fan.

5. A. I had a bad day today.
   B. Why? What happened?
   A. I dropped my new CD player.
6. A. What happened to Charlie?
   B. A dog bit him while he was walking.
7. A. What were you doing when the accident happened?
   B. We were driving over a bridge.
8. A. What happened to Helen?
   B. She tripped and fell on the kitchen floor.
9. A. When did they drop their packages?
   B. While they were walking up the stairs.
10. A. What was Jane doing when she hurt herself?
    B. She was cooking on the barbecue.
11. A. You look upset. What's the matter?
    B. I cut myself while I was chopping.
12. A. What happened to Fred?
    B. He fainted at the bus stop.

Page 98 Exercise K

Listen to each story, and then choose the correct answers to the questions you hear.

William's New Apartment

William is having problems with his new apartment. Yesterday he was very frustrated. It was a hot day, and he wasn't able to open his living room windows. And today he's upset because all the lights in his apartment went out. William is very disappointed. Now he won't be able to cook dinner or watch his favorite programs on TV.

1. Why was William frustrated yesterday?
2. Why is he upset today?
3. Why is he disappointed?

Mr. and Mrs. Clark's New Computer

Mr. and Mrs. Clark are having problems with their new computer. Yesterday they were frustrated because they couldn't assemble the computer easily. And today they're upset because the computer crashed. Mr. and Mrs. Clark are very disappointed. Now they won't be able to send any e-mail to their grandchildren.

4. Why were Mr. and Mrs. Clark frustrated yesterday?
5. Why are they upset today?
6. Why are they disappointed?

Page 102 Exercise E

Listen to the story, and then choose the correct answers to the questions you hear.

Poor Janet!

Last year Janet's teacher said she couldn't dance in the school play because she was too clumsy. Janet was very upset. This year Janet practiced every day, and now she dances much better. Unfortunately, last

week she fell down while she was dancing and she hurt herself. Janet is very disappointed. She won't be able to dance in the play this year.

1. Why was Janet upset last year?
2. What did Janet do this year?
3. What happened while Janet was dancing last week?
4. Why is Janet disappointed?

Page 109 Exercise J

Listen and choose the correct answer.

1. Mr. Lopez, I'm really worried about your eyes.
2. Mrs. Parker, I'm concerned about your heart.
3. I saw my doctor today, and she's concerned about my stomach.
4. Ms. Smith, I'm worried about your blood pressure.
5. Ricky, I'm concerned about your hearing.
6. I saw my doctor today, and he's concerned about my knees.

Page 115 Exercise E

Listen and choose the correct answer.

1. A. What will Betty be doing this afternoon?
   B. She'll be ironing dresses.
2. A. What will Sally and Tom be doing this morning?
   B. They'll be working downtown.
3. A. What will your husband be doing today?
   B. He'll be knitting on the front porch.
4. A. Will you be busy tonight?
   B. Yes, I will. I'll be watching sports.
5. A. Will you and Frank be busy in a half hour?
   B. Yes, we will. We'll be feeding the baby.
6. A. What will Charles be doing later tonight?
   B. He'll be taking a bath.
7. A. Will you and your husband be home this morning?
   B. Yes, we will. We'll be home all morning. We'll be baking cakes.
8. A. Will your daughter be busy this afternoon?
   B. Yes, she will. She'll be doing her homework.
9. A. What will Teddy and Timmy be doing this Sunday morning?
   B. I'm sure they'll be sleeping all morning.
10. A. Will your daughter be home this afternoon?
    B. No, she won't. She'll be skateboarding in the park.
11. A. Will you and your wife be busy this afternoon?
    B. Yes, we will. I think we'll be walking the dog.
12. A. I'm sad that you're leaving.
    B. I know. But don't worry. I'll be thinking about you all the time.

Page 122 Exercise E

Listen to each conversation, and then choose the correct answers to the questions you hear.

Conversation 1

A. I just found this brown wallet on my desk. Is it yours?

B. No. It isn't mine. But it might be John's. He lost his last Tuesday.

A. Thanks. I'll call him right away.

B. I hope it's his. He was very upset when he lost it.

   1. Where was the wallet?

   2. Is the wallet John's?

   3. When did John lose it?

Conversation 2

A. Hello, John? This is Jane. I just found a brown wallet on my desk at work. Is it yours?

B. No. Unfortunately, it isn't mine. Mine is black. But it might be Mary's. She lost hers, too.

A. Okay. I'll call her right away.

B. I hope it's hers. She was very upset when she lost it.

   4. What color is John's wallet?

   5. What did Mary lose at work?

   6. Is the wallet Mary's?

Page 126 Exercise H

Listen and choose the correct response.

1. How was the prom last Saturday?
2. How was your new tuxedo?
3. Was there any good music?
4. How late did you stay?
5. Why did you leave so early?
6. Do you think next year's prom will be better?

Page 129 Exercise L

Listen and choose the person you should call.

1. A. I'm having trouble with my new car!
   B. You should call . . .

2. A. There's water on my bathroom floor!
   B. You should call . . .

3. A. My keys won't open the door lock!
   B. You should call . . .

4. A. My upstairs neighbor lifts weights at two o'clock in the morning!
   B. You should call . . .

5. A. The lights in my kitchen won't go on!
   B. You should call . . .

6. A. Someone stole my bicycle!
   B. You should call . . .

7. A. I can't turn off my kitchen faucet!
   B. You should call . . .

8. A. My computer crashes every day!
   B. You should call . . .

Exercise D Page 133

Listen and choose the correct answers to complete the sentences.

1. Good morning. I'm Doctor Johnson. Today I'll be giving you. . .
2. First, you'll stand on a scale and the nurse will measure . . .
3. Next, the nurse will take your . . .
4. Then you'll go to the lab for some blood tests and . . .
5. Next, we'll go into the examination room and I'll look at your . . .

Correlation Key

Student Text Pages	Activity Workbook Pages	Student Text Pages	Activity Workbook Pages
Chapter 1		**Chapter 8**	
2	2	72	68–70
3	3	73	71
4-5	4–7	74	72–73
6	8	76	74–76
7	9–11	77	77
Chapter 2		79	78
12	12–13	**Check-Up Test**	**79–80**
13	14–15	**Chapter 9**	
14	16–17	84	81–83
15	18–20	85	84–85
Chapter 3		87	86
20	21–23	88-89	87–90
21	24	**Chapter 10**	
23	25–26	94	91–92
24	27	95	93
Check-Up Test	**28–29**	96	94–95
Chapter 4		98-99	96–97
30	30	101	98–100
31	31–33	**Check-Up Test**	**101–102**
33	34	**Chapter 11**	
34	35	106-107	103
35	36–39	108-109	104–106
Chapter 5		111	107–108
40	40	112	109
41	41–42	113	110
42-43	43–46	**Chapter 12**	
45	47–49	116	111
47	50	117-118	112–113
Chapter 6		119	114–115
50	51	120	116
51	52–54	122	117–119
54-55	55–57	**Chapter 13**	
Check-Up Test	**58–59**	126	120
Chapter 7		127	121
62	60	128-129	122–124
63	61	130	125–126
64-65	62–64	131-132	127–131
66	65–66	**Check-Up Test**	**132–133**
67	67		

TEST PREPARATION

Name _____

Date _____ **Class** _____

1

A ASKING PERSONAL INFORMATION QUESTIONS

Choose the sentence with the same meaning.

Example:

What's your age?

- Ⓐ How tall are you?
- Ⓑ What's your weight?
- Ⓒ How old are you?
- Ⓓ Where were you born? Ⓐ Ⓑ ● Ⓓ

1. What's your date of birth?
   - Ⓐ What country are you from?
   - Ⓑ Where were you born?
   - Ⓒ What's your marital status?
   - Ⓓ When were you born?

2. What's your marital status?
   - Ⓐ How much do you weigh?
   - Ⓑ Are you married or single?
   - Ⓒ What country are you from?
   - Ⓓ How tall are you?

3. Where were you born?
   - Ⓐ What's your height?
   - Ⓑ What's your weight?
   - Ⓒ What's your date of birth?
   - Ⓓ What's your place of birth?

4. How tall are you?
   - Ⓐ What's your height?
   - Ⓑ What's your weight?
   - Ⓒ What's your age?
   - Ⓓ What's your nationality?

5. What country are you from?
   - Ⓐ What's your marital status?
   - Ⓑ When were you born?
   - Ⓒ What's your nationality?
   - Ⓓ Are you married or single?

B ANSWERING PERSONAL INFORMATION QUESTIONS

Choose the correct answer.

Example:

What's your zip code?

- Ⓐ 415.
- Ⓑ 10027.
- Ⓒ 027-48-9451.
- Ⓓ #12-G. Ⓐ ● Ⓒ Ⓓ

6. What's your telephone number?
   - Ⓐ 283-73-2851.
   - Ⓑ (215) 627-9382.
   - Ⓒ 97623.
   - Ⓓ 1267-B.

7. What's your height?
   - Ⓐ 155 pounds.
   - Ⓑ 27 years old.
   - Ⓒ Five feet eight inches.
   - Ⓓ Brown.

8. What's your nationality?
   - Ⓐ Mexican.
   - Ⓑ Los Angeles.
   - Ⓒ California.
   - Ⓓ Mexico City.

9. What's your weight?
   - Ⓐ 22214.
   - Ⓑ Five feet three inches.
   - Ⓒ Married.
   - Ⓓ 168 pounds.

10. What's your social security number?
    - Ⓐ 124.
    - Ⓑ 227-53-8716.
    - Ⓒ (617) 372-9106.
    - Ⓓ 33928.

1 Ⓐ Ⓑ Ⓒ Ⓓ   4 Ⓐ Ⓑ Ⓒ Ⓓ   7 Ⓐ Ⓑ Ⓒ Ⓓ   10 Ⓐ Ⓑ Ⓒ Ⓓ

2 Ⓐ Ⓑ Ⓒ Ⓓ   5 Ⓐ Ⓑ Ⓒ Ⓓ   8 Ⓐ Ⓑ Ⓒ Ⓓ

3 Ⓐ Ⓑ Ⓒ Ⓓ   6 Ⓐ Ⓑ Ⓒ Ⓓ   9 Ⓐ Ⓑ Ⓒ Ⓓ

Go to the next page ⟩   **T1** ●

PERSONAL INFORMATION FORM

Name: (1) _____

Street: (2) _____ Apartment: (3) _____

City: (4) _____ State: (5) _____ Zip Code: (6) _____

Social Security Number: (7) _____ Country of Origin: (8) _____

Telephone: (9) _____ E-Mail: (10) _____ Age: (11) _____

Height: (12) _____ Weight: (13) _____ Eye Color: (14) _____ Hair Color: (15) _____

Look at the information. Choose the correct line on the form.

Example:

#201-C
- Ⓐ Line 1
- Ⓑ Line 2
- Ⓒ Line 3
- Ⓓ Line 4

Ⓐ Ⓑ ● Ⓓ

11. 5479 Washington Boulevard
- Ⓐ Line 2
- Ⓑ Line 4
- Ⓒ Line 8
- Ⓓ Line 10

12. China
- Ⓐ Line 1
- Ⓑ Line 2
- Ⓒ Line 8
- Ⓓ Line 10

13. andre27@ail.com
- Ⓐ Line 1
- Ⓑ Line 6
- Ⓒ Line 7
- Ⓓ Line 10

14. 5 ft. 10 in.
- Ⓐ Line 3
- Ⓑ Line 12
- Ⓒ Line 13
- Ⓓ Line 14

15. blue
- Ⓐ Line 12
- Ⓑ Line 13
- Ⓒ Line 14
- Ⓓ Line 15

11 Ⓐ Ⓑ Ⓒ Ⓓ   13 Ⓐ Ⓑ Ⓒ Ⓓ   15 Ⓐ Ⓑ Ⓒ Ⓓ
12 Ⓐ Ⓑ Ⓒ Ⓓ   14 Ⓐ Ⓑ Ⓒ Ⓓ

Go to the next page ⟩

Name _____ **Date** _____

D GRAMMAR IN CONTEXT: Personal Information

Choose the correct answer to complete the conversation.

Example:
What's your _____?
- Ⓐ city
- Ⓑ nationality
- Ⓒ height
- ⬤ name

17. _____ do you spell your last name?
- Ⓐ How
- Ⓑ Who
- Ⓒ Where
- Ⓓ Why

19. What's your _____ number?
- Ⓐ zip
- Ⓑ security
- Ⓒ e-mail
- Ⓓ telephone

21. _____ are you from?
- Ⓐ Where
- Ⓑ When
- Ⓒ Why
- Ⓓ How

23. What's your _____?
- Ⓐ age
- Ⓑ weight
- Ⓒ height
- Ⓓ nationality

16. My name _____ Marie Isabel Fuentes.
- Ⓐ am
- Ⓑ is
- Ⓒ are
- Ⓓ call

18. _____.
- Ⓐ N-A-M-E
- Ⓑ M-A-R-I-A
- Ⓒ I-S-A-B-E-L
- Ⓓ F-U-E-N-T-E-S

20. My phone number is _____.
- Ⓐ 20018
- Ⓑ 317-29-7834
- Ⓒ (627) 442-3862
- Ⓓ #17-H

22. _____ from Guatemala.
- Ⓐ I
- Ⓑ I'm
- Ⓒ My
- Ⓓ You're

24. I'm five _____ four inches.
- Ⓐ feet
- Ⓑ pounds
- Ⓒ tall
- Ⓓ weigh

··

16 Ⓐ Ⓑ Ⓒ Ⓓ   19 Ⓐ Ⓑ Ⓒ Ⓓ   22 Ⓐ Ⓑ Ⓒ Ⓓ

17 Ⓐ Ⓑ Ⓒ Ⓓ   20 Ⓐ Ⓑ Ⓒ Ⓓ   23 Ⓐ Ⓑ Ⓒ Ⓓ

18 Ⓐ Ⓑ Ⓒ Ⓓ   21 Ⓐ Ⓑ Ⓒ Ⓓ   24 Ⓐ Ⓑ Ⓒ Ⓓ

Go to the next page ⟩

Look at the calendar. Choose the correct answer.

2009

January	February	March	April

May **June** **July** **August**

September **October** **November** **December**

Example:

> Today is September 3rd. Today is _____.
>
> Ⓐ Monday
> Ⓑ Wednesday
> Ⓒ Thursday
> Ⓓ Saturday   Ⓐ ● Ⓒ Ⓓ

25. My birthday is March 13th. This year my birthday is on a _____.

Ⓐ Monday
Ⓑ Sunday
Ⓒ Tuesday
Ⓓ Thursday

26. My father's birthday is December 22nd. This year his birthday is on a _____.

Ⓐ Sunday
Ⓑ Monday
Ⓒ Wednesday
Ⓓ Saturday

27. I'm going to start a new job on the first Monday in May. My first day of work is _____.

Ⓐ May 1st
Ⓑ May 2nd
Ⓒ May 5th
Ⓓ May 26th

28. The twelfth day of March this year is on a _____.

Ⓐ Wednesday
Ⓑ Saturday
Ⓒ Sunday
Ⓓ Thursday

29. My sister is going to get married on the second Saturday in June. The wedding is on _____.

Ⓐ June 7th
Ⓑ June 8th
Ⓒ June 14th
Ⓓ June 15th

F CLOZE READING: Providing Information About Family Members

Choose the correct answers to complete the story.

There are six people in my family. My father **is** **am** **are** a cashier. He
● Ⓑ Ⓒ

work **works** **working** ³⁰ in a supermarket. My mother is **a** **an** **the** ³¹ teacher.
Ⓐ Ⓑ Ⓒ Ⓐ Ⓑ Ⓒ

She **He** **It** ³² works in a pre-school. My sister is **with** **in** **from** ³³ college. She's
Ⓐ Ⓑ Ⓒ Ⓐ Ⓑ Ⓒ

study **studies** **studying** ³⁴ medicine. I have two **brother** **brother's** **brothers** ³⁵. One
Ⓐ Ⓑ Ⓒ Ⓐ Ⓑ Ⓒ

brother is eight years old. He's in **high** **elementary** **middle** ³⁶ school. The other brother is
Ⓐ Ⓑ Ⓒ

sixteen years old. He's in **high** **elementary** **middle** ³⁷ school.
Ⓐ Ⓑ Ⓒ

G LISTENING ASSESSMENT: Giving Personal Information

Read and listen to the questions. Then listen to the interview and answer the questions.

38. What's his address?
  Ⓐ 19 Reedville Street.
  Ⓑ 94 Reedville Street.
  Ⓒ 419 Center Street.
  Ⓓ 94 Center Street.

39. When is his birthday?
  Ⓐ May 3rd.
  Ⓑ May 13th.
  Ⓒ May 30th.
  Ⓓ May 31st.

40. How tall is he?
  Ⓐ 5 feet 3 inches.
  Ⓑ 8 feet 5 inches.
  Ⓒ 5 feet 8 inches.
  Ⓓ 5 feet 10 inches.

H MONTHS, DAYS, & DATES

Look at the abbreviation. Write the correct month of the year.

NOV ____November____   JUL _____   JAN _____

AUG _____   JUN _____   FEB _____

MAR _____   APR _____   MAY _____

SEP _____   OCT _____   DEC _____

Look at the abbreviation. Write the correct day of the week.

MON _____   FRI _____   SUN _____

WED _____   SAT _____   TUE _____

THU _____

Write today's date. _____   **Write your date of birth.** _____

30 Ⓐ Ⓑ Ⓒ Ⓓ   33 Ⓐ Ⓑ Ⓒ Ⓓ   36 Ⓐ Ⓑ Ⓒ Ⓓ   39 Ⓐ Ⓑ Ⓒ Ⓓ

31 Ⓐ Ⓑ Ⓒ Ⓓ   34 Ⓐ Ⓑ Ⓒ Ⓓ   37 Ⓐ Ⓑ Ⓒ Ⓓ   40 Ⓐ Ⓑ Ⓒ Ⓓ

32 Ⓐ Ⓑ Ⓒ Ⓓ   35 Ⓐ Ⓑ Ⓒ Ⓓ   38 Ⓐ Ⓑ Ⓒ Ⓓ   **Go to the next page** ⟩

I ORDINAL NUMBERS

Write the correct ordinal number.

second	2nd	seventeenth	_____
ninth	_____	thirty-first	_____
first	_____	fifty-third	_____
twelfth	_____	eighty-fifth	_____

Write the correct word.

6th _____ sixth

15th _____

21st _____

92nd _____

J WRITING ASSESSMENT: Personal Information Form

Fill out the form.

Name: _____

Street: _____ Apartment: _____

City: _____ State: _____ Zip Code: _____

Telephone: _____ E-Mail: _____

Height: _____ Age: _____ Date of Birth: _____ Social Security Number: _____

Hair Color: _____ Eye Color: _____ Country of Origin: _____

Signature: _____ Today's Date: _____

K SPEAKING ASSESSMENT

I can ask and answer these questions:

Ask Answer

☐ ☐ What's your name?
☐ ☐ What's your address?
☐ ☐ What's your telephone number?
☐ ☐ What's your age?
☐ ☐ What's your date of birth?

Ask Answer

☐ ☐ Where are you from?
☐ ☐ What's your social security number?
☐ ☐ What's your height?
☐ ☐ Who are the people in your family?
☐ ☐ What do they do?

STOP

A SCHOOL PERSONNEL & LOCATIONS

Choose the correct answer.

Example:

The _____ is in the classroom.
- Ⓐ custodian
- ● teacher
- Ⓒ security officer
- Ⓓ clerk

1. The _____ is in the library.
   - Ⓐ principal
   - Ⓑ security officer
   - Ⓒ librarian
   - Ⓓ science teacher

2. Our _____ is in the chemistry lab.
   - Ⓐ science teacher
   - Ⓑ English teacher
   - Ⓒ music teacher
   - Ⓓ school nurse

3. The _____ is in her office.
   - Ⓐ driver's ed instructor
   - Ⓑ librarian
   - Ⓒ security officer
   - Ⓓ principal

4. The _____ is in the cafeteria.
   - Ⓐ music teacher
   - Ⓑ custodian
   - Ⓒ clerk
   - Ⓓ security officer

5. The _____ is on the field.
   - Ⓐ principal
   - Ⓑ school nurse
   - Ⓒ P.E. teacher
   - Ⓓ science teacher

6. The _____ is in his office.
   - Ⓐ librarian
   - Ⓑ school nurse
   - Ⓒ clerk
   - Ⓓ guidance counselor

7. The _____ is in her classroom.
   - Ⓐ music teacher
   - Ⓑ English teacher
   - Ⓒ science teacher
   - Ⓓ P.E. teacher

8. The _____ is in the hall.
   - Ⓐ principal
   - Ⓑ driver's ed instructor
   - Ⓒ security officer
   - Ⓓ clerk

9. The _____ is in the parking lot.
   - Ⓐ P.E. teacher
   - Ⓑ driver's ed instructor
   - Ⓒ guidance counselor
   - Ⓓ security officer

10. The _____ is in the school office.
    - Ⓐ teacher
    - Ⓑ school nurse
    - Ⓒ security guard
    - Ⓓ clerk

11. Our _____ is in our classroom.
    - Ⓐ music teacher
    - Ⓑ English teacher
    - Ⓒ math teacher
    - Ⓓ science teacher

1 Ⓐ Ⓑ Ⓒ Ⓓ   4 Ⓐ Ⓑ Ⓒ Ⓓ   7 Ⓐ Ⓑ Ⓒ Ⓓ   10 Ⓐ Ⓑ Ⓒ Ⓓ

2 Ⓐ Ⓑ Ⓒ Ⓓ   5 Ⓐ Ⓑ Ⓒ Ⓓ   8 Ⓐ Ⓑ Ⓒ Ⓓ   11 Ⓐ Ⓑ Ⓒ Ⓓ

3 Ⓐ Ⓑ Ⓒ Ⓓ   6 Ⓐ Ⓑ Ⓒ Ⓓ   9 Ⓐ Ⓑ Ⓒ Ⓓ

Go to the next page

B CLASSROOM INSTRUCTIONS

Choose the correct answer.

Example:

Open your _____.
- (A) ruler
- (B) pencil
- (C) wall
- (D) book

(A) (B) (C) ●

12. Raise your _____.
- (A) seat
- (B) book
- (C) hand
- (D) computer

13. Erase the _____.
- (A) board
- (B) pencil
- (C) pen
- (D) globe

14. Take out a piece of _____.
- (A) map
- (B) dictionary
- (C) book
- (D) paper

15. Please hand in your _____.
- (A) homework
- (B) hand
- (C) chair
- (D) desk

16. Turn off the _____.
- (A) map
- (B) lights
- (C) notebook
- (D) ruler

C COMPUTER COMPONENTS

Look at the picture. Choose the correct word.

17.
- (A) radio
- (B) television
- (C) monitor
- (D) video

19.
- (A) notebook
- (B) printer
- (C) bookcase
- (D) desk

18.
- (A) printer
- (B) dictionary
- (C) typewriter
- (D) keyboard

20.
- (A) mouse
- (B) keyboard
- (C) globe
- (D) map

---

12 (A) (B) (C) (D)

13 (A) (B) (C) (D)

14 (A) (B) (C) (D)

15 (A) (B) (C) (D)

16 (A) (B) (C) (D)

17 (A) (B) (C) (D)

18 (A) (B) (C) (D)

19 (A) (B) (C) (D)

20 (A) (B) (C) (D)

Go to the next page ⟩

D GRAMMAR IN CONTEXT: School Registration

Choose the correct answer to complete the conversation.

21. I want to _____ for an English class.
- Ⓐ teach
- Ⓑ go
- Ⓒ register
- Ⓓ study

22. Okay. Please fill out this _____.
- Ⓐ want ad
- Ⓑ registration form
- Ⓒ job application form
- Ⓓ income tax form

23. With a pen or _____?
- Ⓐ a mouse
- Ⓑ a pencil
- Ⓒ a keyboard
- Ⓓ an eraser

24. A pen. And don't write. Please _____.
- Ⓐ print
- Ⓑ erase
- Ⓒ say
- Ⓓ type

E READING: A Class Schedule

Look at Gloria's class schedule. Choose the correct answer.

Time	Period	Class	Room
8:30-9:15	1st	P.E.	Gym
9:20-10:05	2nd	Math	217
10:10-10:50	3rd	English	115
10:55-11:40	4th	Social Studies	208
12:35-1:20	5th	Health	126
1:25-2:10	6th	Science	130
2:15-3:00	7th	Art	105

Example:

What does she study during fourth period?
- Ⓐ Health.
- Ⓑ Science.
- Ⓒ Social Studies.
- Ⓓ English.   Ⓐ Ⓑ ● Ⓓ

25. What does she study during second period?
- Ⓐ P.E.
- Ⓑ Health.
- Ⓒ Art.
- Ⓓ Math.

26. It's 2:00. What's she studying?
- Ⓐ Social Studies.
- Ⓑ English.
- Ⓒ Science.
- Ⓓ Health.

27. It's 10:30. Where is she?
- Ⓐ In Room 115.
- Ⓑ In the gym.
- Ⓒ In Room 130.
- Ⓓ In Room 105.

28. When does she study in Room 126?
- Ⓐ Third period.
- Ⓑ Fifth perod.
- Ⓒ Sixth period.
- Ⓓ Seventh period.

29. What time does her Science class begin?
- Ⓐ At 8:30.
- Ⓑ At 2:10.
- Ⓒ At 1:25.
- Ⓓ At 1:30.

30. What time does her 7th period class end?
- Ⓐ At 9:15.
- Ⓑ At 2:15.
- Ⓒ In Room 105.
- Ⓓ At 3:00.

. . . .

21 Ⓐ Ⓑ Ⓒ Ⓓ   24 Ⓐ Ⓑ Ⓒ Ⓓ   27 Ⓐ Ⓑ Ⓒ Ⓓ   30 Ⓐ Ⓑ Ⓒ Ⓓ

22 Ⓐ Ⓑ Ⓒ Ⓓ   25 Ⓐ Ⓑ Ⓒ Ⓓ   28 Ⓐ Ⓑ Ⓒ Ⓓ

23 Ⓐ Ⓑ Ⓒ Ⓓ   26 Ⓐ Ⓑ Ⓒ Ⓓ   29 Ⓐ Ⓑ Ⓒ Ⓓ

Go to the next page >   **T9** ●

F CLOZE READING: The Education System

There are many kinds of schools in the education system of the United States. Many young children **go** (A) **goes** (B) **going** (C) to pre-school, but other children **stayed** (A) **stays** (B) **stay** (C) [31] home or go to day-care centers. The **one** (A) **first** (B) **last** (C) [32] year of public school for most children is kindergarten. In some school systems, children go **from** (A) **to** (B) **with** (C) [33] kindergarten for a full day. In other school systems, **they** (A) **we** (B) **I** (C) [34] go to school for **half** (A) **have** (B) **heavy** (C) [35] a day.

After kindergarten, children usually go to school for 12 **days** (A) **months** (B) **years** (C) [36]. They go to elementary school, middle school, and high school. After that, many students

study (A) **studying** (B) **studies** (C) [37] in colleges, technical schools, and other institutions.

G LISTENING ASSESSMENT: Registration Procedures

Read and listen to the questions. Then listen to the conversation and answer the questions.

38. When DOESN'T the school have English classes?
    - (A) On Monday.
    - (B) On Friday.
    - (C) On Wednesday.
    - (D) On Saturday.

39. Where is Wendy going to write her personal information?
    - (A) On her driver's license.
    - (B) On a registration form.
    - (C) On a pen.
    - (D) On a short English test.

40. At what time AREN'T there any classes at this school?
    - (A) 10:00 A.M.
    - (B) 7:30 P.M.
    - (C) 2:00 P.M.
    - (D) 11:30 A.M.

H LEARNING SKILLS: Chronological Order & Steps in a Process

Put the classroom instructions in order.

_____ Write the answer.
_____ Sit down.
__1__ Stand up.
_____ Pick up the chalk.
_____ Go to the board.
_____ Put down the chalk.

Put the computer operations in order.

_____ Do your work.
_____ Insert the software disk.
_____ Eject the disk and turn off the computer.
_____ Open the software program.
_____ Save your work and close the program.
__1__ Turn on the computer.

I WRITING ASSESSMENT

Describe your school. Tell about the people, the classrooms, and other locations. (Use a separate sheet of paper.)

J SPEAKING ASSESSMENT

I can ask and answer these questions:
Ask Answer
☐ ☐ Where is our classroom?
☐ ☐ What's our class schedule?

---

31 (A) (B) (C) (D)   34 (A) (B) (C) (D)   37 (A) (B) (C) (D)   40 (A) (B) (C) (D)

32 (A) (B) (C) (D)   35 (A) (B) (C) (D)   38 (A) (B) (C) (D)

● T10 33 (A) (B) (C) (D)   36 (A) (B) (C) (D)   39 (A) (B) (C) (D)   **STOP**

A FOOD CONTAINERS & QUANTITIES

Example:

We need a _____ of jam.

Ⓐ box   ● jar
Ⓑ loaf   Ⓓ bag

1. Please get a _____ of white bread.

Ⓐ loaf   Ⓒ quart
Ⓑ bunch   Ⓓ bottle

2. I'm looking for a _____ of flour.

Ⓐ pint   Ⓒ loaf
Ⓑ head   Ⓓ bag

3. I need two _____ of whole wheat bread.

Ⓐ loaf   Ⓒ heads
Ⓑ loaves   Ⓓ boxes

4. I need a _____ eggs.

Ⓐ box   Ⓒ dozen
Ⓑ twelve   Ⓓ pound

5. Please give me a _____ of cheese.

Ⓐ can   Ⓒ pint
Ⓑ gallon   Ⓓ pound

B FOOD WEIGHTS & MEASURES: ABBREVIATIONS

6. gal.

Ⓐ quart   Ⓒ gallon
Ⓑ pound   Ⓓ ounce

7. oz.

Ⓐ ounce   Ⓒ pound
Ⓑ quart   Ⓓ pounds

8. qt.

Ⓐ pound   Ⓒ quart
Ⓑ pounds   Ⓓ quarts

9. lbs.

Ⓐ pound   Ⓒ quart
Ⓑ pounds   Ⓓ quarts

10. ounces

Ⓐ ozs.   Ⓒ lb.
Ⓑ oz.   Ⓓ lbs.

11. pound

Ⓐ gal.   Ⓒ lbs.
Ⓑ qt.   Ⓓ lb.

C GRAMMAR IN CONTEXT: Asking About Availability & Location of Items in a Store

12. _____ any bananas today?

Ⓐ Is there
Ⓑ Are there
Ⓒ There is
Ⓓ There are

13. Yes. _____ in the Produce section.

Ⓐ It
Ⓑ It's
Ⓒ They
Ⓓ They're

14. Excuse me. _____ the milk?

Ⓐ Have
Ⓑ Where
Ⓒ Where's
Ⓓ Where are

15. _____ in the Dairy section.

Ⓐ It's
Ⓑ It
Ⓒ They're
Ⓓ They

1 Ⓐ Ⓑ Ⓒ Ⓓ   5 Ⓐ Ⓑ Ⓒ Ⓓ   9 Ⓐ Ⓑ Ⓒ Ⓓ   13 Ⓐ Ⓑ Ⓒ Ⓓ

2 Ⓐ Ⓑ Ⓒ Ⓓ   6 Ⓐ Ⓑ Ⓒ Ⓓ   10 Ⓐ Ⓑ Ⓒ Ⓓ   14 Ⓐ Ⓑ Ⓒ Ⓓ

3 Ⓐ Ⓑ Ⓒ Ⓓ   7 Ⓐ Ⓑ Ⓒ Ⓓ   11 Ⓐ Ⓑ Ⓒ Ⓓ   15 Ⓐ Ⓑ Ⓒ Ⓓ

4 Ⓐ Ⓑ Ⓒ Ⓓ   8 Ⓐ Ⓑ Ⓒ Ⓓ   12 Ⓐ Ⓑ Ⓒ Ⓓ

Go to the next page ➤

Look at the food advertisements. Choose the correct answer.

16. How much are four heads of lettuce?
   Ⓐ $2.00.
   Ⓑ $3.00.
   Ⓒ $4.00.
   Ⓓ $6.00.

17. How much is half a pound of Swiss cheese?
   Ⓐ $17.00.
   Ⓑ $2.50.
   Ⓒ $4.25.
   Ⓓ $8.50.

18. How much are two pounds of Swiss cheese?
   Ⓐ $8.50.
   Ⓑ $17.00.
   Ⓒ $4.25.
   Ⓓ $2.00.

19. How much are four oranges?
   Ⓐ $2.00.
   Ⓑ $1.00.
   Ⓒ $8.00.
   Ⓓ $4.00.

20. How much are a dozen oranges?
   Ⓐ $1.00.
   Ⓑ $2.00.
   Ⓒ $6.00.
   Ⓓ $12.00.

21. How much are two bottles of apple juice?
   Ⓐ Free.
   Ⓑ $1.75.
   Ⓒ $6.98.
   Ⓓ $3.49.

16 Ⓐ Ⓑ Ⓒ Ⓓ   18 Ⓐ Ⓑ Ⓒ Ⓓ   20 Ⓐ Ⓑ Ⓒ Ⓓ

17 Ⓐ Ⓑ Ⓒ Ⓓ   19 Ⓐ Ⓑ Ⓒ Ⓓ   21 Ⓐ Ⓑ Ⓒ Ⓓ

Go to the next page ⟩

E **READING: Food Packaging & Label Information**

For each sentence, choose the correct label.

SELL BY MAR 04	Keep Refrigerated	Serving Size 1 cup (240g) Servings Per Container about 2	Center Pops Up When Original Seal Is Broken
A	**B**	**C**	**D**

22. Do not store at room temperature.
    Ⓐ Ⓑ Ⓒ Ⓓ

23. Contains 2 cups (480g).
    Ⓐ Ⓑ Ⓒ Ⓓ

24. Do not purchase if safety button is up.
    Ⓐ Ⓑ Ⓒ Ⓓ

25. Do not buy after this date.
    Ⓐ Ⓑ Ⓒ Ⓓ

F **READING: A Supermarket Receipt**

Look at the receipt. Choose the correct answer.

26. How much did the eggs cost?
    Ⓐ $2.69.   Ⓒ $2.10.
    Ⓑ $2.00.   Ⓓ $3.00.

27. How many bottles of soda did the person buy?
    Ⓐ One.   Ⓒ Three.
    Ⓑ Two.   Ⓓ Four.

28. How much did the person spend on soda?
    Ⓐ $2.00.   Ⓒ $1.00.
    Ⓑ $3.00.   Ⓓ $6.00.

29. How much does one loaf of bread cost?
    Ⓐ $1.00.   Ⓒ $3.00.
    Ⓑ $2.00.   Ⓓ $6.00.

30. How much do oranges cost at this supermarket?
    Ⓐ $3.00.   Ⓒ 12 for $4.00.
    Ⓑ 3 for $4.00.   Ⓓ 4 for $1.00.

31. How much did the person spend?
    Ⓐ $473.00.   Ⓒ $22.04.
    Ⓑ $2.96.   Ⓓ $25.00.

```
JUMBO SUPERMARKET #473

   LARGE EGGS          2.10
   MILK                2.69
   JAM                 3.25
 2 @ $1.00
   SODA                2.00
 3 @ $2.00
   BREAD               6.00
 2 @ 2 for $3.00
   LETTUCE             3.00
 12 @ 4 for $1.00
   ORANGES             3.00

      TOTAL        $ 22.04
      TENDER       $ 25.00
      CHANGE       $  2.96

Thanks for shopping at JUMBO!
```

G READING: Reading a Menu & Computing Costs

Look at the menu. Choose the correct answer.

SAMMY'S CAFE

SOUP
Vegetable Soup   Cup   1.50   Bowl   2.50
Onion Soup   2.00   3.00

SALAD
Tossed Salad   Small   1.50   Large   3.00

SIDE DISHES
French Fries   2.50   Carrots   2.00
Rice   3.00   Peas   2.00

ENTREES
Chicken   7.00   Spaghetti &
Fish   8.00   Meatballs   6.50
Steak   10.00   Vegetable Stew   7.50

DESSERTS
Pie   3.50   Fresh Strawberries   4.00
Cake   3.50

32. Julia ate at Sammy's Cafe yesterday. She ordered a bowl of vegetable soup and a large salad. How much did she pay?
   Ⓐ $3.00.
   Ⓑ $4.00.
   Ⓒ $5.50.
   Ⓓ $6.00.

33. Ken ordered a small salad, chicken, and rice. How much did he spend?
   Ⓐ $11.50.
   Ⓑ $12.00.
   Ⓒ $12.50.
   Ⓓ $13.00.

34. Sally ate a cup of onion soup, fish, and peas. How much was her bill?
   Ⓐ $11.50.
   Ⓑ $12.50.
   Ⓒ $13.00.
   Ⓓ $12.00.

35. Jeff had a cup of vegetable soup, steak, french fries, and carrots. How much did he spend at the restaurant?
   Ⓐ $16.00.
   Ⓑ $15.50.
   Ⓒ $15.00.
   Ⓓ $14.50.

36. Dora ordered a small salad, vegetable stew, and a piece of cake for dessert. What did she pay?
   Ⓐ $11.50.
   Ⓑ $12.00.
   Ⓒ $12.50.
   Ⓓ $13.00.

37. Ted ordered a bowl of onion soup, chicken, carrots, peas, and fresh strawberries. How much did he pay?
   Ⓐ $16.00.
   Ⓑ $18.00.
   Ⓒ $17.00.
   Ⓓ $17.50.

H LISTENING ASSESSMENT: Ordering a Meal

Read and listen to the questions. Then listen to the conversation and answer the questions.

38. Where is the conversation taking place?
   Ⓐ In a supermarket.
   Ⓑ In a restaurant.
   Ⓒ In a home.
   Ⓓ In a school lunchroom.

39. What is the customer going to have for an appetizer?
   Ⓐ A glass of milk.
   Ⓑ An order of rice.
   Ⓒ The baked chicken.
   Ⓓ A bowl of soup.

40. How many side orders is the customer going to have?
   Ⓐ None.
   Ⓑ One.
   Ⓒ Two.
   Ⓓ Three.

I WRITING ASSESSMENT

What do you usually buy at the supermarket or other food store? How much do you usually spend? Write about it on a separate sheet of paper.

J SPEAKING ASSESSMENT

I can ask and answer these questions:

Ask Answer
☐   ☐   What foods do you like?
☐   ☐   What did you have for breakfast today?
☐   ☐   What did you have for dinner yesterday?

32 Ⓐ Ⓑ Ⓒ Ⓓ   35 Ⓐ Ⓑ Ⓒ Ⓓ   38 Ⓐ Ⓑ Ⓒ Ⓓ
33 Ⓐ Ⓑ Ⓒ Ⓓ   36 Ⓐ Ⓑ Ⓒ Ⓓ   39 Ⓐ Ⓑ Ⓒ Ⓓ
T14   34 Ⓐ Ⓑ Ⓒ Ⓓ   37 Ⓐ Ⓑ Ⓒ Ⓓ   40 Ⓐ Ⓑ Ⓒ Ⓓ

STOP

Name _____

Date _____ Class _____

A SMALL TALK AT WORK & AT SCHOOL

Choose the correct response.

1. What time is the break?
   - Ⓐ It's on Friday.
   - Ⓑ Every morning.
   - Ⓒ It's at 10:30.
   - Ⓓ Five days a week.

2. What's the weather forecast for tomorrow?
   - Ⓐ It's raining.
   - Ⓑ It's going to rain.
   - Ⓒ It rained.
   - Ⓓ It didn't rain.

3. I'm really tired today.
   - Ⓐ Congratulations!
   - Ⓑ That's great!
   - Ⓒ I'm glad to hear that.
   - Ⓓ I'm sorry to hear that.

4. It's very hot in the building today.
   - Ⓐ I agree. It's hot.
   - Ⓑ I agree. It isn't very hot.
   - Ⓒ I disagree. It's hot.
   - Ⓓ I disagree. It's very hot.

5. What kind of TV shows do you like?
   - Ⓐ You like news programs.
   - Ⓑ I like news programs.
   - Ⓒ I play baseball.
   - Ⓓ I like adventure movies.

6. Did you see the president on TV last night?
   - Ⓐ No, he wasn't.
   - Ⓑ No, you didn't.
   - Ⓒ Yes, I did.
   - Ⓓ Yes, you did.

7. Do you think Mr. Lawson will give a math test tomorrow?
   - Ⓐ I agree.
   - Ⓑ I disagree.
   - Ⓒ I think she will.
   - Ⓓ I think he will.

8. Do you think it'll rain tomorrow?
   - Ⓐ Maybe it will, and maybe it won't.
   - Ⓑ Maybe we will, and maybe we won't.
   - Ⓒ Maybe you will, and maybe you won't.
   - Ⓓ Maybe I will, and maybe I won't.

9. Do you think we'll have to work overtime?
   - Ⓐ Maybe we did, and maybe we didn't.
   - Ⓑ Maybe we do, and maybe we don't.
   - Ⓒ Maybe we will, and maybe we won't.
   - Ⓓ Maybe we are, and maybe we aren't.

10. Are you going out for lunch today?
    - Ⓐ No. I'm going to a restaurant.
    - Ⓑ No. I'm going to eat in my office.
    - Ⓒ Yes. I'm going to eat in my office.
    - Ⓓ Yes. I'm not going out for lunch.

---

1 Ⓐ Ⓑ Ⓒ Ⓓ   4 Ⓐ Ⓑ Ⓒ Ⓓ   7 Ⓐ Ⓑ Ⓒ Ⓓ   10 Ⓐ Ⓑ Ⓒ Ⓓ

2 Ⓐ Ⓑ Ⓒ Ⓓ   5 Ⓐ Ⓑ Ⓒ Ⓓ   8 Ⓐ Ⓑ Ⓒ Ⓓ

3 Ⓐ Ⓑ Ⓒ Ⓓ   6 Ⓐ Ⓑ Ⓒ Ⓓ   9 Ⓐ Ⓑ Ⓒ Ⓓ

Go to the next page ⟩

B GRAMMAR IN CONTEXT: Invitations & Offers

Choose the correct answer to complete the conversations.

11. Would _____ like some milk?
- Ⓐ you'll
- Ⓑ you
- Ⓒ you're
- Ⓓ you do

12. _____ I'd love some.
- Ⓐ Yes. Thanks.
- Ⓑ No. Thanks.
- Ⓒ No thank you.
- Ⓓ Please don't.

13. Would you like to _____ with me after work today?
- Ⓐ will have dinner
- Ⓑ has dinner
- Ⓒ having dinner
- Ⓓ have dinner

14. I'm sorry. _____
- Ⓐ You can't.
- Ⓑ You can.
- Ⓒ I can't.
- Ⓓ I can.

15. _____ you sure?
- Ⓐ Do
- Ⓑ Does
- Ⓒ Is
- Ⓓ Are

16. Yes. _____ work late.
- Ⓐ I have to
- Ⓑ I have
- Ⓒ You have
- Ⓓ I'm

17. _____ like to go sailing with me?
- Ⓐ Did you
- Ⓑ Did I
- Ⓒ Would you
- Ⓓ Would I

18. No, _____ .
- Ⓐ I don't
- Ⓑ I don't think so
- Ⓒ I think so
- Ⓓ I think

19. Why _____?
- Ⓐ don't
- Ⓑ doesn't
- Ⓒ no
- Ⓓ not

20. _____ get seasick.
- Ⓐ He might
- Ⓑ I'm
- Ⓒ I'm afraid I might
- Ⓓ You're afraid

....

11 Ⓐ Ⓑ Ⓒ Ⓓ   14 Ⓐ Ⓑ Ⓒ Ⓓ   17 Ⓐ Ⓑ Ⓒ Ⓓ   20 Ⓐ Ⓑ Ⓒ Ⓓ

12 Ⓐ Ⓑ Ⓒ Ⓓ   15 Ⓐ Ⓑ Ⓒ Ⓓ   18 Ⓐ Ⓑ Ⓒ Ⓓ

13 Ⓐ Ⓑ Ⓒ Ⓓ   16 Ⓐ Ⓑ Ⓒ Ⓓ   19 Ⓐ Ⓑ Ⓒ Ⓓ

Go to the next page ⟩

C GRAMMAR IN CONTEXT: Asking for Clarification

Choose the correct answer to complete the conversations.

21. Will the train _____ soon?
- Ⓐ will arrive
- Ⓑ arrive
- Ⓒ going to arrive
- Ⓓ is going to arrive

22. Yes. _____ in five minutes.
- Ⓐ Arrive
- Ⓑ Going to arrive
- Ⓒ It arrive
- Ⓓ It'll arrive

23. _____
- Ⓐ In five minutes?
- Ⓑ It'll arrive?
- Ⓒ Yes, it will.
- Ⓓ No?

24. Yes. _____
- Ⓐ It's going to.
- Ⓑ You'll arrive.
- Ⓒ I will.
- Ⓓ That's right.

25. My birthday is _____ May 3rd.
- Ⓐ from
- Ⓑ with
- Ⓒ on
- Ⓓ at

26. May _____?
- Ⓐ who
- Ⓑ what
- Ⓒ why
- Ⓓ how

27. Where _____ you live?
- Ⓐ do
- Ⓑ does
- Ⓒ is
- Ⓓ are

28. I live _____ apartment 3-C.
- Ⓐ on
- Ⓑ with
- Ⓒ for
- Ⓓ in

29. _____ 3-G?
- Ⓐ Did you live
- Ⓑ Do you live
- Ⓒ Did you say
- Ⓓ Do you say

30. _____
- Ⓐ Yes. 3-G.
- Ⓑ Yes. 3-C.
- Ⓒ No. 3-G.
- Ⓓ No. 3-C.

21 Ⓐ Ⓑ Ⓒ Ⓓ   24 Ⓐ Ⓑ Ⓒ Ⓓ   27 Ⓐ Ⓑ Ⓒ Ⓓ   30 Ⓐ Ⓑ Ⓒ Ⓓ

22 Ⓐ Ⓑ Ⓒ Ⓓ   25 Ⓐ Ⓑ Ⓒ Ⓓ   28 Ⓐ Ⓑ Ⓒ Ⓓ

23 Ⓐ Ⓑ Ⓒ Ⓓ   26 Ⓐ Ⓑ Ⓒ Ⓓ   29 Ⓐ Ⓑ Ⓒ Ⓓ

Go to the next page ➤

D CLOZE READING: Small Talk at Work

Choose the correct answers to complete the story.

"Small talk" [of (A)] [at (●)] [when (C)] work is very important. Co-workers [talk (A)] [talks (B)] [talking (C)] ³¹ with each other about many different things. They talk about [my (A)] [your (B)] [their (C)] ³² favorite movies and TV programs. They talk [above (A)] [about (B)] [with (C)] ³³ music and sports. [Much (A)] [Many (B)] [Co-workers (C)] ³⁴ people also talk about the weather. Some subjects [don't (A)] [aren't (B)] [isn't (C)] ³⁵ very good for "small talk" in some countries, but in other countries [this (A)] [that (B)] [these (C)] ³⁶ subjects are very common. For example, questions about a person's salary or the [price (A)] [receipt (B)] [how much (C)] ³⁷ of a person's home are common in some countries but very unusual in other countries.

E LISTENING ASSESSMENT: An Invitation

Read and listen to the questions. Then listen to the conversation and answer the questions.

38. What day is it?
    - Ⓐ Tuesday.
    - Ⓑ Wednesday.
    - Ⓒ Thursday.
    - Ⓓ We don't know.

39. What are they going to do tomorrow?
    - Ⓐ Make dinner.
    - Ⓑ Have dinner.
    - Ⓒ Go to a class.
    - Ⓓ Go to a meeting.

40. Where are they going to meet?
    - Ⓐ At the restaurant.
    - Ⓑ At the computer class.
    - Ⓒ On Wednesday.
    - Ⓓ At the person's office.

F WRITING ASSESSMENT

Describe your plans for the weekend. What are you going to do? What might you do? Write about it on a separate sheet of paper.

G SPEAKING ASSESSMENT

I can ask and answer these questions:

Ask Answer
- ☐ ☐ How do you like the weather today?
- ☐ ☐ What's the weather forecast for tomorrow?
- ☐ ☐ What kind of TV shows do you like?
- ☐ ☐ What kind of music do you like?
- ☐ ☐ What did you do last weekend?
- ☐ ☐ What are you going to do next weekend?

31 Ⓐ Ⓑ Ⓒ Ⓓ   34 Ⓐ Ⓑ Ⓒ Ⓓ   37 Ⓐ Ⓑ Ⓒ Ⓓ   40 Ⓐ Ⓑ Ⓒ Ⓓ
32 Ⓐ Ⓑ Ⓒ Ⓓ   35 Ⓐ Ⓑ Ⓒ Ⓓ   38 Ⓐ Ⓑ Ⓒ Ⓓ
33 Ⓐ Ⓑ Ⓒ Ⓓ   36 Ⓐ Ⓑ Ⓒ Ⓓ   39 Ⓐ Ⓑ Ⓒ Ⓓ

STOP

A SMALL TALK AT WORK & AT SCHOOL

Choose the correct response.

1. How do you like our new boss?
   I think she's _____ our old boss.
   - Ⓐ friendly
   - Ⓑ friendlier
   - Ⓒ friendlier than
   - Ⓓ more friendly

2. What do you think about our new English teacher?
   I think he's _____ our old teacher.
   - Ⓐ nicer
   - Ⓑ nicer than
   - Ⓒ more nice than
   - Ⓓ more nice

3. What's your favorite kind of music?
   Rock music. I think it's _____ other kinds of music.
   - Ⓐ better than
   - Ⓑ good than
   - Ⓒ more good than
   - Ⓓ more better than

4. The weather today is beautiful.
   I agree. It's _____ yesterday.
   - Ⓐ nice
   - Ⓑ nicer
   - Ⓒ nicer than
   - Ⓓ more nice than

5. I think your computer is newer than mine.
   It is. Mine is newer than _____.
   - Ⓐ my
   - Ⓑ mine
   - Ⓒ your
   - Ⓓ yours

6. Our math class isn't very interesting any more.
   I agree. It _____ more interesting.
   - Ⓐ to be used
   - Ⓑ used to be
   - Ⓒ used be to
   - Ⓓ was to be

7. Should I work overtime today or tomorrow?
   _____ work overtime today.
   - Ⓐ You think I should
   - Ⓑ You should I think
   - Ⓒ I think you should
   - Ⓓ I should you think

8. My locker isn't as clean as your locker.
   You're right. Mine _____ yours.
   - Ⓐ is cleaner than
   - Ⓑ isn't cleaner than
   - Ⓒ is as clean as
   - Ⓓ isn't as clean as

9. You know, the food in the cafeteria isn't as good as it used to be.
   I agree. The food _____.
   - Ⓐ is better now
   - Ⓑ are better now
   - Ⓒ used to be
   - Ⓓ used to be better

10. I think our science class is more interesting than our history class.
    I disagree. I think history _____ science.
    - Ⓐ isn't as interesting
    - Ⓑ isn't as interesting as
    - Ⓒ is more interesting
    - Ⓓ is more interesting than

1 Ⓐ Ⓑ Ⓒ Ⓓ   4 Ⓐ Ⓑ Ⓒ Ⓓ   7 Ⓐ Ⓑ Ⓒ Ⓓ   10 Ⓐ Ⓑ Ⓒ Ⓓ

2 Ⓐ Ⓑ Ⓒ Ⓓ   5 Ⓐ Ⓑ Ⓒ Ⓓ   8 Ⓐ Ⓑ Ⓒ Ⓓ

3 Ⓐ Ⓑ Ⓒ Ⓓ   6 Ⓐ Ⓑ Ⓒ Ⓓ   9 Ⓐ Ⓑ Ⓒ Ⓓ

Go to the next page

Choose the correct answer to complete the conversations.

11. _____ a very nice bicycle.
- Ⓐ That
- Ⓑ That's
- Ⓒ This
- Ⓓ These

12. _____
- Ⓐ It is that.
- Ⓑ It's a bicycle.
- Ⓒ Thanks.
- Ⓓ You're welcome.

13. _____ fast?
- Ⓐ Is it
- Ⓑ It is
- Ⓒ Are they
- Ⓓ They are

14. Yes. It's _____ my old bicycle.
- Ⓐ faster
- Ⓑ faster than
- Ⓒ more fast
- Ⓓ more

15. These cookies _____.
- Ⓐ is delicious
- Ⓑ more delicious
- Ⓒ much more delicious
- Ⓓ are delicious

16. Thanks. My new recipe is _____ my old one.
- Ⓐ much better than
- Ⓑ much better
- Ⓒ more good
- Ⓓ better

17. Your apartment _____.
- Ⓐ nicer than
- Ⓑ is nicer than
- Ⓒ is very nice
- Ⓓ are very nice

18. Thank you. Do you like _____?
- Ⓐ my sofa is new
- Ⓑ my sofa is newer
- Ⓒ my new sofa
- Ⓓ newer sofa

19. Yes. It's _____ than your old one.
- Ⓐ attractive
- Ⓑ more attractive
- Ⓒ much attractive
- Ⓓ much more

20. I think so, too. It's also _____ comfortable.
- Ⓐ much
- Ⓑ good
- Ⓒ better
- Ⓓ more

11 Ⓐ Ⓑ Ⓒ Ⓓ   14 Ⓐ Ⓑ Ⓒ Ⓓ   17 Ⓐ Ⓑ Ⓒ Ⓓ   20 Ⓐ Ⓑ Ⓒ Ⓓ

12 Ⓐ Ⓑ Ⓒ Ⓓ   15 Ⓐ Ⓑ Ⓒ Ⓓ   18 Ⓐ Ⓑ Ⓒ Ⓓ

13 Ⓐ Ⓑ Ⓒ Ⓓ   16 Ⓐ Ⓑ Ⓒ Ⓓ   19 Ⓐ Ⓑ Ⓒ Ⓓ   Go to the next page ⟶

C GRAMMAR IN CONTEXT: Appropriate Language in Social Situations

Choose the correct answer to complete the conversations.

21. _____ You're stepping on my foot.
- Ⓐ Excuse me.
- Ⓑ Excuse.
- Ⓒ You excuse me.
- Ⓓ I excuse you.

22. Oh. _____
- Ⓐ You apologize.
- Ⓑ I apologize.
- Ⓒ You're apologizing.
- Ⓓ I'm apologizing.

23. That's okay. _____
- Ⓐ Think.
- Ⓑ Don't think.
- Ⓒ Worry about it.
- Ⓓ Don't worry about it.

24. _____
- Ⓐ It's very sorry.
- Ⓑ We're very sorry.
- Ⓒ I'm really sorry.
- Ⓓ You're really sorry.

25. You _____. Is something wrong?
- Ⓐ are looking
- Ⓑ look sad
- Ⓒ sad
- Ⓓ the matter

26. Yes. I have _____.
- Ⓐ some bad news
- Ⓑ some bad
- Ⓒ some good news
- Ⓓ some good

27. What _____?
- Ⓐ happen
- Ⓑ happened
- Ⓒ happening
- Ⓓ going to happen

28. My husband _____ yesterday.
- Ⓐ lose job
- Ⓑ lost job
- Ⓒ lose his job
- Ⓓ lost his job

29. I'm _____ that.
- Ⓐ sorry
- Ⓑ sorry to
- Ⓒ sorry to hear
- Ⓓ sorry hear

30. _____
- Ⓐ Thank you.
- Ⓑ I agree.
- Ⓒ I disagree.
- Ⓓ You're sorry.

. . . .

21 Ⓐ Ⓑ Ⓒ Ⓓ   24 Ⓐ Ⓑ Ⓒ Ⓓ   27 Ⓐ Ⓑ Ⓒ Ⓓ   30 Ⓐ Ⓑ Ⓒ Ⓓ

22 Ⓐ Ⓑ Ⓒ Ⓓ   25 Ⓐ Ⓑ Ⓒ Ⓓ   28 Ⓐ Ⓑ Ⓒ Ⓓ

23 Ⓐ Ⓑ Ⓒ Ⓓ   26 Ⓐ Ⓑ Ⓒ Ⓓ   29 Ⓐ Ⓑ Ⓒ Ⓓ   Go to the next page

D CLOZE READING: A Thank-You Note

Choose the correct answers to complete the note.

Dear Alan,

Thank you [with (A) | **for** ● | by (C)] the wonderful dinner yesterday. [They (A) | It (B) | I (C)] ^{31} was

delicious. The vegetable soup [were (A) | was (B) | did (C)] ^{32} great, the hamburgers [were (A) | was (B) | are (C)] ^{33}

excellent, and the [potatoes (A) | carrots (B) | chili (C)] ^{34} was also very good. In fact, I think your recipe

is much [good (A) | more good (B) | better (C)] ^{35} than [my (A) | mine (B) | me (C)] ^{36}.

Thank you again. Next time [I'll (A) | I'm (B) | I (C)] ^{37} invite you to MY place for dinner.

Sincerely,

Natalie

E LISTENING ASSESSMENT: Expressing Opinions

Read and listen to the questions. Then listen to the conversation and answer the questions.

38. What do they disagree about?
    - (A) The buildings.
    - (B) The streets.
    - (C) The people.
    - (D) The weather.

39. What do they agree about?
    - (A) The people and the buildings.
    - (B) The buildings and the parks.
    - (C) The streets and the buildings.
    - (D) The streets and the people.

40. Which opinion do they probably agree about?
    - (A) The buildings in other cities are more interesting.
    - (B) The people in other cities are friendlier.
    - (C) The streets in other cities are cleaner.
    - (D) The parks in other cities are more beautiful.

F WRITING ASSESSMENT

Compare two different places you know. Write about the streets, the buildings, the weather, the people, and life in these two places. (Use a separate sheet of paper.)

G SPEAKING ASSESSMENT

I can ask and answer these questions:

Ask Answer
- ☐ ☐ What's your favorite food?
- ☐ ☐ How do you like my new _____?
- ☐ ☐ What do you think about our English class?
- ☐ ☐ What's your opinion about life in our city?

31 (A) (B) (C) (D)   34 (A) (B) (C) (D)   37 (A) (B) (C) (D)   40 (A) (B) (C) (D)
32 (A) (B) (C) (D)   35 (A) (B) (C) (D)   38 (A) (B) (C) (D)
33 (A) (B) (C) (D)   36 (A) (B) (C) (D)   39 (A) (B) (C) (D)

A SHOPPING REQUESTS & LOCATING ITEMS

These people are shopping in a department store. Where is each person shopping?
Choose the correct department.

Ex: "I'm looking for a new TV."
  Ⓐ Appliances   ● Home
                     Entertainment
  Ⓑ Jewelry   Ⓓ Customer Service

1. "Do you have this tie in blue?"
  Ⓐ Jewelry   Ⓒ Men's Clothing
  Ⓑ Furniture   Ⓓ Women's Clothing

2. "Is this dishwasher the best one you have?"
  Ⓐ Furniture   Ⓒ Customer Service
  Ⓑ Appliances   Ⓓ Home
                     Entertainment

3. "I want to buy a ring."
  Ⓐ Jewelry   Ⓒ Home
                     Entertainment
  Ⓑ Furniture   Ⓓ Appliances

4. "We need a new kitchen table."
  Ⓐ Furniture   Ⓒ Cosmetics
  Ⓑ Jewelry   Ⓓ Appliances

5. "Do you have any longer dresses?"
  Ⓐ Jewelry   Ⓒ Women's Clothing
  Ⓑ Furniture   Ⓓ Home
                     Entertainment

6. "I want to return this item."
  Ⓐ Rest Rooms   Ⓒ Appliances
  Ⓑ Cosmetics   Ⓓ Customer Service

7. "I'm looking for a shirt for my little boy."
  Ⓐ Toys   Ⓒ Men's Clothing
  Ⓑ Appliances   Ⓓ Children's Clothing

B UNDERSTANDING ATM INSTRUCTIONS

Read the ATM instruction. Choose the correct answer.

8. Enter the amount in dollars and cents.
  Ⓐ OKAY
  Ⓑ 4761
  Ⓒ $50.00
  Ⓓ ENTER

9. Choose a transaction: WITHDRAWAL
  Ⓐ Insert card.
  Ⓑ Get money.
  Ⓒ Put in money.
  Ⓓ Press ENTER.

10. Choose a transaction: DEPOSIT
  Ⓐ Put in money.
  Ⓑ Press OKAY.
  Ⓒ Get money.
  Ⓓ Insert card.

11. Enter your PIN (Personal Indentification Number)
  Ⓐ $0.00
  Ⓑ $50.00
  Ⓒ 4761
  Ⓓ P-I-N

12. Balance Inquiry
  Ⓐ Choose another account.
  Ⓑ Last Deposit: $463.12
  Ⓒ Last Withdrawal: $100.00
  Ⓓ Funds available: $1,241.63

13. Do you want to make another transaction?
  Ⓐ Enter your PIN.
  Ⓑ Press YES or NO.
  Ⓒ Enter the amount.
  Ⓓ Insert your card.

1 Ⓐ Ⓑ Ⓒ Ⓓ   5 Ⓐ Ⓑ Ⓒ Ⓓ   9   Ⓐ Ⓑ Ⓒ Ⓓ   13 Ⓐ Ⓑ Ⓒ Ⓓ

2 Ⓐ Ⓑ Ⓒ Ⓓ   6 Ⓐ Ⓑ Ⓒ Ⓓ   10 Ⓐ Ⓑ Ⓒ Ⓓ

3 Ⓐ Ⓑ Ⓒ Ⓓ   7 Ⓐ Ⓑ Ⓒ Ⓓ   11 Ⓐ Ⓑ Ⓒ Ⓓ

4 Ⓐ Ⓑ Ⓒ Ⓓ   8 Ⓐ Ⓑ Ⓒ Ⓓ   12 Ⓐ Ⓑ Ⓒ Ⓓ

C INTERPRETING A CHECK

		1024
		(1) _____
Pay to the order of ___**(2)**_____	$ **(3)**_____	
(4)_____Dollars		
For **(5)**_____	**(6)**_____	

057009345 200042534 1024

Look at the information. Where should you write it? Choose the correct line on the check.

14. Savemax Clothing Store

- Ⓐ Line 2
- Ⓑ Line 4
- Ⓒ Line 5
- Ⓓ Line 6

15. 36.40

- Ⓐ Line 1
- Ⓑ Line 3
- Ⓒ Line 4
- Ⓓ Line 6

16. Nov. 22, 2009

- Ⓐ Line 1
- Ⓑ Line 3
- Ⓒ Line 5
- Ⓓ Line 6

17. pants & belt

- Ⓐ Line 2
- Ⓑ Line 4
- Ⓒ Line 5
- Ⓓ Line 6

18. *Pedro Martinez*

- Ⓐ Line 3
- Ⓑ Line 4
- Ⓒ Line 5
- Ⓓ Line 6

19. Thirty-six and 40/100................................

- Ⓐ Line 2
- Ⓑ Line 3
- Ⓒ Line 4
- Ⓓ Line 5

D GRAMMAR IN CONTEXT: Problems with Purchases; Returning an Item

Ex: _____ help you?
- Ⓐ Can you
- Ⓑ You can
- ⬤ May I
- Ⓓ I may

21. Is there a _____ with it?
- Ⓐ problem
- Ⓑ matter
- Ⓒ wrong
- Ⓓ something

23. Do you have your _____?
- Ⓐ DVD player
- Ⓑ check
- Ⓒ receipt
- Ⓓ ATM card

20. Yes. _____ return this DVD player.
- Ⓐ I want
- Ⓑ I want to
- Ⓒ You want
- Ⓓ You want to

22. Yes. It's _____. It doesn't work.
- Ⓐ a DVD player
- Ⓑ wrong
- Ⓒ the matter
- Ⓓ broken

24. Yes. _____
- Ⓐ Here I am.
- Ⓑ Here they are.
- Ⓒ I don't have it.
- Ⓓ Here it is.

14 Ⓐ Ⓑ Ⓒ Ⓓ   17 Ⓐ Ⓑ Ⓒ Ⓓ   20 Ⓐ Ⓑ Ⓒ Ⓓ   23 Ⓐ Ⓑ Ⓒ Ⓓ

15 Ⓐ Ⓑ Ⓒ Ⓓ   18 Ⓐ Ⓑ Ⓒ Ⓓ   21 Ⓐ Ⓑ Ⓒ Ⓓ   24 Ⓐ Ⓑ Ⓒ Ⓓ

16 Ⓐ Ⓑ Ⓒ Ⓓ   19 Ⓐ Ⓑ Ⓒ Ⓓ   22 Ⓐ Ⓑ Ⓒ Ⓓ   Go to the next page >

E GRAMMAR IN CONTEXT: Problems with Purchases; Exchanging an Item

25. I'd like to _____ this cell phone.
- Ⓐ give
- Ⓑ return
- Ⓒ take
- Ⓓ call

26. What's the _____ with it?
- Ⓐ matter
- Ⓑ wrong
- Ⓒ why
- Ⓓ what's wrong

27. _____ small enough.
- Ⓐ They aren't
- Ⓑ Aren't they
- Ⓒ It isn't
- Ⓓ Isn't it

28. Do you want to _____ it for a smaller one?
- Ⓐ return
- Ⓑ buy
- Ⓒ give
- Ⓓ exchange

29. _____ a smaller one?
- Ⓐ You do have
- Ⓑ Do you have
- Ⓒ Have you
- Ⓓ You do

30. Yes. This used to be the _____ one, but now we have a smaller one.
- Ⓐ smallest
- Ⓑ more small
- Ⓒ more smallest
- Ⓓ much small

31. Then I think _____ exchange it.
- Ⓐ I like
- Ⓑ you like
- Ⓒ you'd like to
- Ⓓ I'd like to

32. Okay. Go to the Electronics _____. Somebody there will help you.
- Ⓐ store
- Ⓑ furniture
- Ⓒ department
- Ⓓ entertainment

F CLOZE READING: Store Sales

Choose the correct answers to complete the story.

Many department stores [has Ⓐ / **have ●** / does Ⓒ] sales. When there is a sale, you can

[give Ⓐ / take Ⓑ / buy Ⓒ] [33] items at special low [prices Ⓐ / receipts Ⓑ / departments Ⓒ] [34]. Sometimes you

need a coupon for a sale. You can find coupons in the [radio Ⓐ / newspaper Ⓑ / TV Ⓒ] [35]. Many

stores send ads with coupons to people's homes through the [store Ⓐ / mail Ⓑ / service Ⓒ] [36].

Look for sales at stores [near Ⓐ / with Ⓑ / far Ⓒ] [37] you. You can save a lot of money!

....

25 Ⓐ Ⓑ Ⓒ Ⓓ   29 Ⓐ Ⓑ Ⓒ Ⓓ   33 Ⓐ Ⓑ Ⓒ Ⓓ   37 Ⓐ Ⓑ Ⓒ Ⓓ

26 Ⓐ Ⓑ Ⓒ Ⓓ   30 Ⓐ Ⓑ Ⓒ Ⓓ   34 Ⓐ Ⓑ Ⓒ Ⓓ

27 Ⓐ Ⓑ Ⓒ Ⓓ   31 Ⓐ Ⓑ Ⓒ Ⓓ   35 Ⓐ Ⓑ Ⓒ Ⓓ

28 Ⓐ Ⓑ Ⓒ Ⓓ   32 Ⓐ Ⓑ Ⓒ Ⓓ   36 Ⓐ Ⓑ Ⓒ Ⓓ

Go to the next page ▷

G LISTENING ASSESSMENT: Returning Items

Read and listen to the questions. Then listen to the conversation and answer the questions.

38. How many items does the person want to return?
- Ⓐ One.
- Ⓑ Two.
- Ⓒ Three.
- Ⓓ Four.

39. What's the matter with the shirt?
- Ⓐ It's big.
- Ⓑ It's large.
- Ⓒ It's small.
- Ⓓ It's blue.

40. Where is the conversation taking place?
- Ⓐ In the elevator.
- Ⓑ At the Customer Service Counter.
- Ⓒ On the first floor.
- Ⓓ In the Men's Clothing Department.

H WRITING ASSESSMENT: Fill Out the Check

Pay this bill. Fill out the check.

Metrovision
Cable TV

Cable TV Service	$24.95
Past Due	0.00
DUE NOW	**$24.95**

1024

Pay to the order of _____ $_____

_____ Dollars

For _____ _____

057009345 200042534 1024

I LEARNING SKILL: Steps in a Process

Put the ATM instructions in order.

_____ Choose a transaction.

_____ Take your money, your card, and your receipt.

__1__ Insert your ATM card.

_____ Enter the amount in dollars and cents.

_____ Enter your PIN on the keypad and press ENTER.

_____ Check the amount and press OKAY.

J SPEAKING ASSESSMENT

I can ask and answer these questions:

Ask Answer
- ☐ ☐ Where do you shop for clothing?
- ☐ ☐ Why do you shop there?

Ask Answer
- ☐ ☐ In your opinion, what's the best place to buy a TV or other home entertainment product?
- ☐ ☐ Why do you think so?

38 Ⓐ Ⓑ Ⓒ Ⓓ   39 Ⓐ Ⓑ Ⓒ Ⓓ   40 Ⓐ Ⓑ Ⓒ Ⓓ

STOP

A SCHEDULES

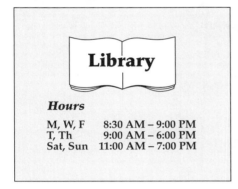

Clinic

Mon–Fri	8:30 – 7:30
Sat	8:30 – 5:30
Sun	Closed

Post Office

Mon–Fri	8:00 – 5:00
Sat	8:00 – 1:00
Sun	Closed

Motor Vehicles Department

Open
M–Th	8:30 – 4:30
Fri	8:30 – 7:00
Sat	9:00 – 12:00
Closed Sunday	

Library

Hours
M, W, F	8:30 AM – 9:00 PM
T, Th	9:00 AM – 6:00 PM
Sat, Sun	11:00 AM – 7:00 PM

UNITED STATES POSTAL SERVICE

COLLECTION TIMES

| Monday – Friday | Saturday | Sunday |
| 9:00 AM 2:00 PM 11:30 AM | 1:00 PM | Holiday |

Location of Express Mail Drop: 250 Adams Street
For information call: (800) ASK–USPS

Look at the schedules. Choose the correct answer.

Example:

What time does the clinic open on Saturday?
- Ⓐ At 5:30.
- Ⓑ At 7:30.
- ● At 8:30.
- Ⓓ It's closed.

1. What time does the clinic close on Wednesday?
- Ⓐ At 5:30.
- Ⓑ At 7:30.
- Ⓒ At 8:30.
- Ⓓ It's closed.

2. What time does the post office open on Tuesday?
- Ⓐ At 8:00.
- Ⓑ At 1:00.
- Ⓒ At 3:00.
- Ⓓ At 5:00.

3. How many hours is the Motor Vehicles Department open on Monday?
- Ⓐ Three.
- Ⓑ Eight.
- Ⓒ Nine.
- Ⓓ Ten.

4. What time does the library close on Thursday?
- Ⓐ At 6:00 AM.
- Ⓑ At 9:00 AM.
- Ⓒ At 6:00 PM.
- Ⓓ At 9:00 PM.

5. On which day is the Motor Vehicles Department open later in the evening?
- Ⓐ Saturday.
- Ⓑ Monday.
- Ⓒ Thursday.
- Ⓓ Friday.

6. What time do they pick up the mail on weekday afternoons?
- Ⓐ At 2:00 PM.
- Ⓑ At 1:00 PM.
- Ⓒ At 11:30 AM.
- Ⓓ At 9:00 AM.

7. How many times do they pick up the mail on weekday mornings?
- Ⓐ One.
- Ⓑ Two.
- Ⓒ Three.
- Ⓓ Four.

....

1 Ⓐ Ⓑ Ⓒ Ⓓ   3 Ⓐ Ⓑ Ⓒ Ⓓ   5 Ⓐ Ⓑ Ⓒ Ⓓ   7 Ⓐ Ⓑ Ⓒ Ⓓ

2 Ⓐ Ⓑ Ⓒ Ⓓ   4 Ⓐ Ⓑ Ⓒ Ⓓ   6 Ⓐ Ⓑ Ⓒ Ⓓ

Look at the map. Choose the correct place.

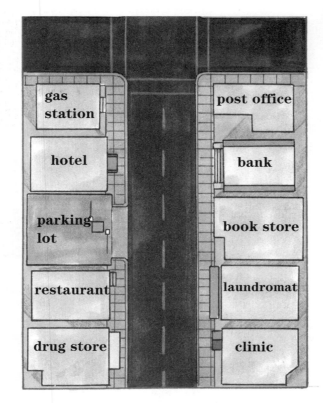

Example:

It's across from the hotel.
- Ⓐ The gas station.
- Ⓑ The bank.
- Ⓒ The parking lot.
- Ⓓ The post office.   Ⓐ ⬤ Ⓒ Ⓓ

8. It's next to the clinic.
   - Ⓐ The drug store.
   - Ⓑ The book store.
   - Ⓒ The laundromat.
   - Ⓓ The restaurant.

9. It's on the east side of the street, between the bank and the laundromat.
   - Ⓐ The post office.
   - Ⓑ The parking lot.
   - Ⓒ The hotel.
   - Ⓓ The book store.

10. It's on the west side of the street, north of the hotel.
    - Ⓐ The parking lot.
    - Ⓑ The gas station.
    - Ⓒ The bank.
    - Ⓓ The post office.

11. It's on the east side of the street, south of the laundromat.
    - Ⓐ The clinic.
    - Ⓑ The restaurant.
    - Ⓒ The drug store.
    - Ⓓ The book store.

8 Ⓐ Ⓑ Ⓒ Ⓓ   9 Ⓐ Ⓑ Ⓒ Ⓓ   10 Ⓐ Ⓑ Ⓒ Ⓓ   11 Ⓐ Ⓑ Ⓒ Ⓓ

C READING: A Bus Schedule

Look at the bus schedule.
Choose the correct answer.

Example:

Where does this bus route start?
- (A) Russell Avenue.
- (B) Metro Plaza.
- (C) Custis Drive.
- (D) King Street. (A) (B) (C) ●

Route 18A				
King Street	Braddock Road	Russell Avenue	Custis Drive	Metro Plaza
Weekdays				
5:40 AM	5:51	6:01	6:06	6:13
6:00	6:11	6:21	6:26	6:33
6:20	6:31	6:41	6:46	6:53
6:40	6:51	7:01	7:06	7:13
7:00	7:11	7:21	7:26	7:33
7:20	7:31	7:41	7:46	7:53
7:40	7:51	8:01	8:06	8:13
8:00	8:11	8:21	8:26	8:33
8:20	8:31	8:41	8:46	8:53
8:40	8:51	9:01	9:06	9:13
9:00	9:11	9:21	9:26	9:33
10:05	10:15	10:25	10:30	-
11:05	11:15	11:25	11:30	-
12:05 PM	12:15	12:25	12:30	-
1:05	1:15	1:25	1:30	-
2:05	2:15	2:25	2:30	-
3:05	3:16	3:26	3:31	3:38
3:50	4:01	4:11	4:16	4:23
4:10	4:21	4:31	4:36	4:43
4:30	4:41	4:51	4:56	5:03
4:50	5:01	5:11	5:16	5:23
5:10	5:21	5:31	5:36	5:43
5:30	5:41	5:51	5:56	6:03
5:50	6:01	6:11	6:16	6:23
6:10	6:21	6:31	6:36	6:43
6:30	6:41	6:51	6:56	7:03
6:50	7:01	7:11	7:16	7:23

12. Where does this bus route end?
- (A) King Street.
- (B) Braddock Road.
- (C) Russell Avenue.
- (D) Metro Plaza.

13. What time does the first bus leave King Street?
- (A) 5:40 AM.
- (B) 6:13 AM.
- (C) 6:50 PM.
- (D) 7:23 PM.

14. What time does the last bus arrive at Custis Drive?
- (A) 6:06 AM.
- (B) 6:13 AM.
- (C) 7:16 PM.
- (D) 7:23 PM.

15. When does the 7:00 AM bus arrive at Russell Avenue?
- (A) 7:00 AM.
- (B) 7:11 AM.
- (C) 7:11 PM.
- (D) 7:21 AM.

16. Which bus doesn't stop at Metro Plaza?
- (A) The 6:00 AM bus from King Street.
- (B) The 9:00 AM bus from King Street.
- (C) The 1:05 PM bus from King Street.
- (D) The 3:05 PM bus from King Street.

17. How long does it take any bus to go from King Street to Metro Plaza?
- (A) 11 minutes.
- (B) 12 minutes.
- (C) 30 minutes.
- (D) 33 minutes.

18. It's 12:30 PM, and you're at the bus stop on King Street. How long do you have to wait for the bus?
- (A) 1 hour.
- (B) 35 minutes.
- (C) 30 minutes.
- (D) 5 minutes.

....

12 (A) (B) (C) (D)   14 (A) (B) (C) (D)   16 (A) (B) (C) (D)   18 (A) (B) (C) (D)

13 (A) (B) (C) (D)   15 (A) (B) (C) (D)   17 (A) (B) (C) (D)

Go to the next page ⟩

D HIGHWAY & TRAFFIC SIGNS & SYMBOLS

Choose the correct sign.

A

B

C

D

Example:

There are train tracks ahead.
Watch out for trains.

Ⓐ Ⓑ ● Ⓓ

19. No left turn.

Ⓐ Ⓑ Ⓒ Ⓓ

20. There's a crosswalk ahead.
Watch out for pedestrians.

Ⓐ Ⓑ Ⓒ Ⓓ

21. When you enter this road, let the other
cars already on the road go first.

Ⓐ Ⓑ Ⓒ Ⓓ

E POLICE COMMANDS & TRAFFIC SIGNS

Choose the correct sign.

A

B

C

D

Example:

"Stop! You can't enter this street from
here!"

Ⓐ Ⓑ Ⓒ ●

22. "Slow down! You're in a school zone!"

Ⓐ Ⓑ Ⓒ Ⓓ

23. "You can't make a U-turn here!"

Ⓐ Ⓑ Ⓒ Ⓓ

24. "Turn around! You're going in the wrong
direction!"

Ⓐ Ⓑ Ⓒ Ⓓ

....

T30

19 Ⓐ Ⓑ Ⓒ Ⓓ

20 Ⓐ Ⓑ Ⓒ Ⓓ

21 Ⓐ Ⓑ Ⓒ Ⓓ

22 Ⓐ Ⓑ Ⓒ Ⓓ

23 Ⓐ Ⓑ Ⓒ Ⓓ

24 Ⓐ Ⓑ Ⓒ Ⓓ

Go to the next page ▷

F **GRAMMAR IN CONTEXT: Postal Services**

Example:

I want to send this _____ to Texas.

- Ⓐ postcard
- ⬤ package
- Ⓒ letter
- Ⓓ envelope

25. Do you want to send it _____ surface mail or air mail?

- Ⓐ for
- Ⓑ with
- Ⓒ by
- Ⓓ from

26. _____ recommend?

- Ⓐ What does it
- Ⓑ What do I
- Ⓒ What does he
- Ⓓ What do you

27. Let's see. It weighs eight _____ and eleven ounces.

- Ⓐ inches
- Ⓑ pounds
- Ⓒ feet
- Ⓓ miles

28. How much will it _____?

- Ⓐ cost
- Ⓑ costs
- Ⓒ send
- Ⓓ sends

29. _____ $4.50 surface mail or $7.25 air mail.

- Ⓐ I'll cost
- Ⓑ You'll cost
- Ⓒ It'll cost
- Ⓓ They'll cost

30. _____ will it take to get there by surface mail?

- Ⓐ How much
- Ⓑ How many
- Ⓒ How short
- Ⓓ How long

31. About ten _____.

- Ⓐ miles
- Ⓑ ounces
- Ⓒ days
- Ⓓ feet

32. I think I'll send it by surface mail. And I'd also like a book of first-class _____, please.

- Ⓐ postcards
- Ⓑ stamps
- Ⓒ money orders
- Ⓓ aerogrammes

All right.

25 Ⓐ Ⓑ Ⓒ Ⓓ   28 Ⓐ Ⓑ Ⓒ Ⓓ   31 Ⓐ Ⓑ Ⓒ Ⓓ

26 Ⓐ Ⓑ Ⓒ Ⓓ   29 Ⓐ Ⓑ Ⓒ Ⓓ   32 Ⓐ Ⓑ Ⓒ Ⓓ

27 Ⓐ Ⓑ Ⓒ Ⓓ   30 Ⓐ Ⓑ Ⓒ Ⓓ

Go to the next page ⟩

G CLOZE READING: Simple Written Directions

Choose the correct answers to complete the directions.

Here are directions from our school to my apartment. Walk west along School Street

for	to	next
Ⓐ	⬤	Ⓒ

Pond Road and

drive	for	turn
Ⓐ	Ⓑ	Ⓒ

³³ right. Walk north on Pond Road three

blocks	walks	turns
Ⓐ	Ⓑ	Ⓒ

³⁴ to River Street and turn left. Walk west on River Street and you'll

see my apartment building

in	on	with
Ⓐ	Ⓑ	Ⓒ

³⁵ the right,

across	around	between
Ⓐ	Ⓑ	Ⓒ

³⁶ a bank

and a bakery.

H LISTENING ASSESSMENT: Compass Directions

Read and listen to the questions. Then listen to the conversation and answer the questions.

37. In which direction is the post office?
    - Ⓐ North.
    - Ⓑ South.
    - Ⓒ East.
    - Ⓓ West.

38. In which direction is the library?
    - Ⓐ North.
    - Ⓑ South.
    - Ⓒ East.
    - Ⓓ West.

39. In which direction is the shopping mall?
    - Ⓐ North.
    - Ⓑ South.
    - Ⓒ East.
    - Ⓓ West.

40. In which direction is the zoo?
    - Ⓐ North.
    - Ⓑ South.
    - Ⓒ East.
    - Ⓓ West.

I WRITING ASSESSMENT

Draw a map and write simple directions from your school to your home. (Use a separate sheet of paper.)

J SPEAKING ASSESSMENT

I can ask and answer these questions:

Ask Answer

☐ ☐ Can you tell me how to get to the post office?

☐ ☐ Could you please tell me how to get to the airport from here?

☐ ☐ Would you please tell me how to get to the nearest hospital?

☐ ☐ What's the best way to get to your home from here?

· ·

33 Ⓐ Ⓑ Ⓒ Ⓓ   35 Ⓐ Ⓑ Ⓒ Ⓓ   37 Ⓐ Ⓑ Ⓒ Ⓓ   39 Ⓐ Ⓑ Ⓒ Ⓓ

34 Ⓐ Ⓑ Ⓒ Ⓓ   36 Ⓐ Ⓑ Ⓒ Ⓓ   38 Ⓐ Ⓑ Ⓒ Ⓓ   40 Ⓐ Ⓑ Ⓒ Ⓓ

STOP

Name _____

Date _____ Class _____

A HELP WANTED ADS

Look at the Help Wanted ads. Choose the correct answer.

	CASHIERS
Iding	FT & PT. $11/hr. Exper. pref.
ot.	Apply in person. M-F 9am-1pm.
utilites	Save-Mart. 2640 Central Ave.

CASHIERS
FT & PT. $11/hr. Exper. pref.
Apply in person. M-F 9am-1pm.
Save-Mart. 2640 Central Ave.

DRIVERS
FT. 40 hr/wk. Excel. salary.
Exper. req. A-1 Car Rental
Company. Must have own trans.
Call 714-293-4444.

OFFICE ASSISTANT
PT. M-F eves 6-8. Sat. 9-11am.
Excel. typing skills req. Tip Top
Travel. Call Sheila at 714-592-7000.

DATA ENTRY CLERK
FT entry-level position.
Req. good math skills. Will train.
Excel. benefits. Lifeco Insurance.
Call 714-938-3350.

Example:

Which company only has a part-time job available?

Ⓐ Save-Mart.
Ⓑ A-1 Car Rental Company.
Ⓒ Lifeco Insurance.
Ⓓ Tip Top Travel.　　Ⓐ Ⓑ Ⓒ ●

1. Which ad gives information about the salary?

Ⓐ The ad for drivers.
Ⓑ The ad for an office assistant.
Ⓒ The ad for cashiers.
Ⓓ The ad for a data entry clerk.

2. Victor wants to apply for a job as a driver. What does he have to do?

Ⓐ He has to call Save-Mart.
Ⓑ He has to call 714-938-3350.
Ⓒ He has to call 714-592-7000.
Ⓓ He has to call 714-293-4444.

3. How many hours per week does the office assistant work?

Ⓐ 10 hours per week.
Ⓑ 12 hours per week.
Ⓒ 14 hours per week.
Ⓓ 40 hours per week.

4. What does a person need for the job at Lifeco Insurance?

Ⓐ Math skills.
Ⓑ Excellent typing skills.
Ⓒ Experience as a cashier.
Ⓓ Transportation.

5. Which sentence ISN'T true about the jobs at Save-Mart?

Ⓐ Experience is preferred.
Ⓑ A person doesn't have to call first to apply for a job.
Ⓒ Experience is required.
Ⓓ There are part-time and full-time jobs available.

1 Ⓐ Ⓑ Ⓒ Ⓓ　　3 Ⓐ Ⓑ Ⓒ Ⓓ　　5 Ⓐ Ⓑ Ⓒ Ⓓ

2 Ⓐ Ⓑ Ⓒ Ⓓ　　4 Ⓐ Ⓑ Ⓒ Ⓓ

Go to the next page >

Example:

Tell me about _____ skills.

- Ⓐ my
- ● your
- Ⓒ its
- Ⓓ their

6. I _____ use a cash register, and I _____ how to take inventory.
   - Ⓐ know . . . can
   - Ⓑ know . . . know
   - Ⓒ can . . . can
   - Ⓓ can . . . know

7. Do you have any _____ as a cashier?
   - Ⓐ work
   - Ⓑ work experience
   - Ⓒ help wanted
   - Ⓓ experience preferred

8. Yes. I _____ a cashier in my last job.
   - Ⓐ work
   - Ⓑ worked
   - Ⓒ was
   - Ⓓ am

9. Where _____ work and for how long?
   - Ⓐ you did
   - Ⓑ did you
   - Ⓒ you were
   - Ⓓ were you

10. I worked at the Save-Rite Market _____ two years.
    - Ⓐ for
    - Ⓑ from
    - Ⓒ during
    - Ⓓ in

C **DESCRIBING A WORK SCHEDULE**

Look at Maria Perdomo's work schedule. Choose the correct answer.

WORK SCHEDULE		SEPTEMBER					
	SUN	MON	TUE	WED	THU	FRI	SAT
Start	12:00 PM	8:30 AM	8:30 AM		9:15 AM	9:15 AM	7:45 AM
End	9:00 PM	2:30 PM	2:30 PM		6:15 PM	6:15 PM	4:45 PM

Example:

How many days does she work this week?
- Ⓐ Four.
- Ⓑ Five.
- ● Six.
- Ⓓ Seven.

11. Which day is her day off?
    - Ⓐ Monday.
    - Ⓑ Wednesday.
    - Ⓒ Saturday.
    - Ⓓ Sunday.

12. What time does she begin work on Thursday?
    - Ⓐ 9:15 AM.
    - Ⓑ 6:15 PM.
    - Ⓒ 8:30 AM.
    - Ⓓ 12:00 PM.

13. What time does she finish work on Tuesday?
    - Ⓐ 8:30 AM.
    - Ⓑ 6:15 PM.
    - Ⓒ 4:45 PM.
    - Ⓓ 2:30 PM.

14. How many hours does she work on Friday?
    - Ⓐ Six.
    - Ⓑ Eight.
    - Ⓒ Nine.
    - Ⓓ Ten.

15. What is the total number of hours she works this week?
    - Ⓐ 35.
    - Ⓑ 40.
    - Ⓒ 48.
    - Ⓓ 50.

6 Ⓐ Ⓑ Ⓒ Ⓓ 9 Ⓐ Ⓑ Ⓒ Ⓓ 12 Ⓐ Ⓑ Ⓒ Ⓓ 15 Ⓐ Ⓑ Ⓒ Ⓓ
7 Ⓐ Ⓑ Ⓒ Ⓓ 10 Ⓐ Ⓑ Ⓒ Ⓓ 13 Ⓐ Ⓑ Ⓒ Ⓓ
8 Ⓐ Ⓑ Ⓒ Ⓓ 11 Ⓐ Ⓑ Ⓒ Ⓓ 14 Ⓐ Ⓑ Ⓒ Ⓓ

Go to the next page →

Name _____ Date _____

D **GRAMMAR IN CONTEXT: Calling In Sick & Late; Requesting a Schedule Change**

Ex: Hello, Ms. Pratt. This is Ted Simon. I'm afraid I _____ come to work today.
- ● can't
- Ⓑ can
- Ⓒ have
- Ⓓ can to

17. _____ feel very sick.
- Ⓐ I
- Ⓑ I'm
- Ⓒ You
- Ⓓ You're

16. What's the _____, Ted?
- Ⓐ with you
- Ⓑ sick
- Ⓒ why
- Ⓓ matter

18. Okay. _____ come to work today.
- Ⓐ Don't have to
- Ⓑ You don't have to
- Ⓒ I have to
- Ⓓ I don't have to

19. Ms. Pratt? This is Debbie Simpson. _____ be late for work this morning.
- Ⓐ I'll arrive
- Ⓑ I'm going to arrive
- Ⓒ I'm going to
- Ⓓ I'm going

What happened?

20. My bus _____ a flat tire. I _____ wait for another bus.
- Ⓐ has . . . have to
- Ⓑ have . . . has to
- Ⓒ has . . . has to
- Ⓓ have . . . have to

Don't worry about it, Debbie. I'll see you when you get here.

Excuse me, Mr. Hunter. Can I possibly change my work schedule for next week?

21. What _____ change?
- Ⓐ you want
- Ⓑ do you want
- Ⓒ you want to
- Ⓓ do you want to

22. I'd like to change my _____ to Tuesday. I have to take my children to the doctor that day.
- Ⓐ off day
- Ⓑ day off
- Ⓒ sick day
- Ⓓ weekend day

23. I understand. Yes, you have my _____.
- Ⓐ application
- Ⓑ schedule
- Ⓒ permission
- Ⓓ change

16 Ⓐ Ⓑ Ⓒ Ⓓ   18 Ⓐ Ⓑ Ⓒ Ⓓ   20 Ⓐ Ⓑ Ⓒ Ⓓ   22 Ⓐ Ⓑ Ⓒ Ⓓ
17 Ⓐ Ⓑ Ⓒ Ⓓ   19 Ⓐ Ⓑ Ⓒ Ⓓ   21 Ⓐ Ⓑ Ⓒ Ⓓ   23 Ⓐ Ⓑ Ⓒ Ⓓ   **T35**

ACCIDENT REPORT

1. Name of Employee / Injured Person

2. Job Title

3. Sex

4. Date of Birth

5. SSN

6. Day, Date, & Time of Occurrence

7. Location of Accident

8. Description of Injury (Part of body injured & nature of injury)

9. What was the accident and how did it occur?

10. Safety Equipment or Procedures Being Used at Time of Accident

11. Contributing Factors (e.g., lack of training)

12. What do you recommend to prevent this accident in the future?

13. Name & Position of Witness(es)

14. Name of Physician

15. Employee's Signature

Look at the information. Choose the correct line on the form.

24. Shipping department
    - (A) Line 2
    - (B) Line 6
    - (C) Line 7
    - (D) Line 8

25. Friday, 2/10/08, 4:15 PM
    - (A) Line 3
    - (B) Line 4
    - (C) Line 5
    - (D) Line 6

26. I broke my right foot.
    - (A) Line 7
    - (B) Line 8
    - (C) Line 9
    - (D) Line 11

27. A big box fell off the forklift and dropped on my foot.
    - (A) Line 7
    - (B) Line 8
    - (C) Line 9
    - (D) Line 10

28. Michael Fuentes, stock clerk
    - (A) Line 1
    - (B) Line 2
    - (C) Line 10
    - (D) Line 13

29. The company should buy stronger protective shoes for employees in the shipping department.
    - (A) Line 12
    - (B) Line 11
    - (C) Line 10
    - (D) Line 9

24 (A) (B) (C) (D)   26 (A) (B) (C) (D)   28 (A) (B) (C) (D)

25 (A) (B) (C) (D)   27 (A) (B) (C) (D)   29 (A) (B) (C) (D)

Go to the next page ⟩

F READING: A Paycheck Stub

APRIL COMPANY		RIZAL, J.		EMP. NO. 60159
PAY PERIOD ENDING	RATE	HOURS		EARNINGS
120508	9.97	40		398.80

FED TAX	33.59		EARNINGS	398.80
FICA/MED	26.47		TAXES	70.92
STATE TAX	10.86		DEDUCTIONS	43.16
HEALTH	43.16			
			NET PAY	284.72

APRIL COMPANY   CHECK NO. 16889
DATE ISSUED 121808

Pay to   JOSE RIZAL $284.72

TWO HUNDRED EIGHTY-FOUR DOLLARS AND SEVENTY-TWO CENTS

Dee Boss

Look at the paycheck stub. Choose the correct answer.

30. What is Mr. Rizal's salary?
    - Ⓐ 40 hours a week.
    - Ⓑ $9.97 per hour.
    - Ⓒ $284.72 per year.
    - Ⓓ $398.80 per year.

31. How much did he earn during this pay period?
    - Ⓐ $398.80.
    - Ⓑ $9.97.
    - Ⓒ $40.00.
    - Ⓓ $284.72.

32. How much was the deduction for state taxes?
    - Ⓐ $43.16.
    - Ⓑ $33.59.
    - Ⓒ $26.47.
    - Ⓓ $10.86.

33. How much pay did Mr. Rizal take home after deductions?
    - Ⓐ $398.80.
    - Ⓑ $284.72.
    - Ⓒ $40 per hour.
    - Ⓓ $9.97 per hour.

G CLOZE READING: Nonverbal Behavior at the Job Interview

Choose the correct answers to complete the story.

The information you give at a job interview is important, but your nonverbal behavior is also important. You should dress [neat (A) / **neatly (B)** / sloppily (C)]. Shake hands [to (A) / with (B) / for (C)] [34] the interviewer firmly. A firm handshake shows that you are [friend (A) / friends (B) / friendly (C)] [35] and confident. Make "eye contact." Look at the interviewer [direct (A) / directly (B) / director (C)] [36]. Don't speak too quickly, and don't speak too loudly or too [softly (A) / softer (B) / soft (C)] [37]. And don't forget to smile!

H LISTENING ASSESSMENT: A Job Interview

Read and listen to the questions. Then listen to the conversation and answer the questions.

38. What kind of position is the person applying for?
   - Ⓐ A job as a cashier.
   - Ⓑ An office position.
   - Ⓒ A position in a supermarket.
   - Ⓓ A job in a computer factory.

39. Where is the conversation taking place?
   - Ⓐ At the Larsen Real Estate Agency.
   - Ⓑ At the Citywide Supermarket.
   - Ⓒ At Landmark Data Management.
   - Ⓓ At the Johnson Insurance Company.

40. How many years of work experience does the applicant have?
   - Ⓐ 1 year.
   - Ⓑ 2 years.
   - Ⓒ 3 years.
   - Ⓓ 6 years.

I WRITING: A Job Application Form

Complete this form about yourself.

APPLICATION FOR EMPLOYMENT

Name _____ Social Security Number _____

Address _____
        Street   City   State   ZIP Code

Phone No. (   ) _____ Age (if under 21) _____ Birth Date (if under 21) ___/___/___
                                                                          Month Day Year

Position Desired _____ Salary Desired _____ Date you can start _____

EDUCATION

Type of School	Name	Location	Years Completed	Graduated?
High School				
College				
Other				

EMPLOYMENT (Start with present or most recent employer)

Date (Month/Year)	Name and Address of Employer	Position	Salary
From To			
From To			
From To			

Date _____ Signature _____

J SPEAKING ASSESSMENT

I can ask and answer these questions:

Ask Answer
- ☐ ☐ What kind of job are you looking for?
- ☐ ☐ Tell me about your skills and abilities.
- ☐ ☐ Tell me about your previous education.
- ☐ ☐ Tell me a little about yourself.

Ask Answer
- ☐ ☐ Are you currently employed?
- ☐ ☐ Tell me about your work history.
- ☐ ☐ Why do you want to work here?
- ☐ ☐ Do you have any questions about the position?

STOP

A FIRST-AID KIT

Choose the correct answer.

1. He took _____ for his headache.
   - Ⓐ a cotton ball
   - Ⓑ aspirin
   - Ⓒ a band-aid
   - Ⓓ adhesive tape

2. I cut my finger. Could you please get _____ from the first-aid kit?
   - Ⓐ a band-aid
   - Ⓑ a piece of paper
   - Ⓒ a cotton ball
   - Ⓓ an ACE bandage

3. You should put some _____ on that cut.
   - Ⓐ ice cream
   - Ⓑ toothpaste
   - Ⓒ aspirin
   - Ⓓ antibiotic ointment

4. I'm going to clean the wound with _____.
   - Ⓐ adhesive tape
   - Ⓑ a napkin
   - Ⓒ an antiseptic cleansing wipe
   - Ⓓ a band-aid

5. The doctor used _____ to take the splinter out of my finger.
   - Ⓐ a knife
   - Ⓑ a screwdriver
   - Ⓒ scissors
   - Ⓓ tweezers

6. The school nurse wrapped my ankle with _____.
   - Ⓐ an ACE bandage
   - Ⓑ adhesive tape
   - Ⓒ toilet paper
   - Ⓓ an antiseptic cleansing wipe

7. You scraped your knee. I'm going to put on _____.
   - Ⓐ adhesive tape
   - Ⓑ a sterile gauze dressing pad
   - Ⓒ a cotton ball
   - Ⓓ an ACE bandage

8. Attach the gauze pad with _____.
   - Ⓐ adhesive tape
   - Ⓑ an ACE bandage
   - Ⓒ a string
   - Ⓓ a band-aid

1 Ⓐ Ⓑ Ⓒ Ⓓ   3 Ⓐ Ⓑ Ⓒ Ⓓ   5 Ⓐ Ⓑ Ⓒ Ⓓ   7 Ⓐ Ⓑ Ⓒ Ⓓ

2 Ⓐ Ⓑ Ⓒ Ⓓ   4 Ⓐ Ⓑ Ⓒ Ⓓ   6 Ⓐ Ⓑ Ⓒ Ⓓ   8 Ⓐ Ⓑ Ⓒ Ⓓ

Choose the correct answer to complete the conversations.

Emergency Operator.

9. I want to _____ a robbery!
   (A) do
   (B) catch
   (C) report
   (D) make

10. _____ the address?
    (A) When is
    (B) Who is
    (C) How is
    (D) What is

241 Central Avenue, Apartment 5.

11. And please tell me _____.
    (A) who happened
    (B) when it's happening
    (C) what happened
    (D) what's going to happen

12. Burglars broke into our apartment while we _____.
    (A) working
    (B) were working
    (C) work
    (D) works

13. Okay. We'll send a patrol car _____.
    (A) right away
    (B) yesterday
    (C) next month
    (D) every day

Thank you.

This is the Fairfax Emergency Center. You're on a recorded line.

14. We need _____ at 650 Main Street!
    (A) an emergency
    (B) a prescription
    (C) a first-aid kit
    (D) an ambulance

What's the emergency?

15. I think my father is having _____.
    (A) a very bad cold
    (B) an upset stomach
    (C) a heart attack
    (D) an earache

An emergency vehicle is on the way.

Thank you.

9 (A) (B) (C) (D)   11 (A) (B) (C) (D)   13 (A) (B) (C) (D)   15 (A) (B) (C) (D)

10 (A) (B) (C) (D)   12 (A) (B) (C) (D)   14 (A) (B) (C) (D)   Go to the next page ⟩

C GRAMMAR IN CONTEXT: Describing a Suspect's Physical Characteristics to the Police

16. Can you describe his _____?
- (A) width
- (B) height
- (C) length
- (D) weight

17. He was about six feet _____.
- (A) long
- (B) high
- (C) tall
- (D) height

18. What was his _____?
- (A) with
- (B) width
- (C) wait
- (D) weight

19. He weighed about 160 _____.
- (A) pounds
- (B) feet
- (C) inches
- (D) yards

20. What _____ was his hair?
- (A) length
- (E) color
- (C) look
- (D) weight

21. It was dark _____.
- (A) thin
- (B) short
- (C) long
- (D) brown

22. Can you describe his _____?
- (A) wear
- (B) wearing
- (C) clothing
- (D) wore

23. He was wearing a red _____ and a pair of gray _____.
- (A) pants . . . shoes
- (B) pants . . . shirt
- (C) shirt . . . pants
- (D) shoes . . . socks

D READING: Warning Labels on Household Products

Choose the correct warning label for each instruction.

Do not use with other household chemicals.	Avoid direct contact. Wear rubber gloves.	Harmful if swallowed.	Avoid prolonged breathing of vapors.
A	B	C	D

24. Do not eat or drink.
- (A) (B) (C) (D)

26. Use only in well-ventilated areas. Avoid fumes.
- (A) (B) (C) (D)

25. Do not get on skin.
- (A) (B) (C) (D)

27. Do not mix together with other products.
- (A) (B) (C) (D)

. . . .

16 (A) (B) (C) (D)   19 (A) (B) (C) (D)   22 (A) (B) (C) (D)   25 (A) (B) (C) (D)

17 (A) (B) (C) (D)   20 (A) (B) (C) (D)   23 (A) (B) (C) (D)   26 (A) (B) (C) (D)

18 (A) (B) (C) (D)   21 (A) (B) (C) (D)   24 (A) (B) (C) (D)   27 (A) (B) (C) (D)

Go to the next page ⟩ T41

E READING: First Aid Procedures

Choose the correct medical procedure for each emergency.

Cover the area with a cool wet cloth or put in cool water.	Try to remove stinger. Clean wound and apply cold cloth. Get medical help if there is itching, swelling, or if the person is dizzy, nauseous, or can't breathe.	Apply direct pressure with a clean cloth or sterile dressing directly on the wound.	If the victim cannot speak, breathe, or cough, ask for someone to call 911 and then perform the Heimlich maneuver.
A	**B**	**C**	**D**

28. bleeding

    Ⓐ Ⓑ Ⓒ Ⓓ

29. choking

    Ⓐ Ⓑ Ⓒ Ⓓ

30. bee sting

    Ⓐ Ⓑ Ⓒ Ⓓ

31. minor burn

    Ⓐ Ⓑ Ⓒ Ⓓ

F LEARNING SKILL: Categorizing Words; Word Sets

Choose the correct answer.

32. Which word isn't a *color*?
   - Ⓐ blue
   - Ⓑ shirt
   - Ⓒ white
   - Ⓓ brown

33. Which word doesn't describe *weight*?
   - Ⓐ heavy
   - Ⓑ fat
   - Ⓒ light
   - Ⓓ short

34. Which word isn't a *form of transportation*?
   - Ⓐ telephone
   - Ⓑ airplane
   - Ⓒ train
   - Ⓓ bus

35. Which word isn't a *season*?
   - Ⓐ spring
   - Ⓑ summer
   - Ⓒ snowing
   - Ⓓ winter

36. Which word isn't a *month*?
   - Ⓐ May
   - Ⓑ Monday
   - Ⓒ August
   - Ⓓ June

37. Which word doesn't describe *height*?
   - Ⓐ heavy
   - Ⓑ tall
   - Ⓒ short
   - Ⓓ medium height

G LISTENING ASSESSMENT: An Emergency Call

Read and listen to the questions. Then listen to the conversation and answer the questions.

38. When did the person fall?
   - Ⓐ While she was on a trip.
   - Ⓑ While she was in her apartment.
   - Ⓒ While she was on the phone.
   - Ⓓ While she was walking down the stairs.

39. What's their address?
   - Ⓐ 13 East Street.
   - Ⓑ 13 West Street.
   - Ⓒ 30 East Street.
   - Ⓓ 30 West Street.

40. Where is their apartment?
   - Ⓐ On the 5th floor.
   - Ⓑ On the 6th floor.
   - Ⓒ Apartment 6-C.
   - Ⓓ Apartment 6-G.

H WRITING ASSESSMENT: Fill Out the Form

Name _____

Height _____ Weight _____

Hair Color _____ Eye Color _____

I SPEAKING ASSESSMENT

I can ask and answer these questions:

Ask Answer
- ☐ ☐ What's your height?
- ☐ ☐ What's your hair color?
- ☐ ☐ What color are your eyes?
- ☐ ☐ What are you wearing today?

28 Ⓐ Ⓑ Ⓒ Ⓓ   31 Ⓐ Ⓑ Ⓒ Ⓓ   35 Ⓐ Ⓑ Ⓒ Ⓓ   38 Ⓐ Ⓑ Ⓒ Ⓓ

29 Ⓐ Ⓑ Ⓒ Ⓓ   32 Ⓐ Ⓑ Ⓒ Ⓓ   36 Ⓐ Ⓑ Ⓒ Ⓓ   39 Ⓐ Ⓑ Ⓒ Ⓓ

30 Ⓐ Ⓑ Ⓒ Ⓓ   33 Ⓐ Ⓑ Ⓒ Ⓓ   37 Ⓐ Ⓑ Ⓒ Ⓓ   40 Ⓐ Ⓑ Ⓒ Ⓓ

34 Ⓐ Ⓑ Ⓒ Ⓓ

STOP

A HOUSING ADS

Look at the classified ads for housing. Choose the correct answer.

2 BR 1 BA, d/w, $950 incl util. 273-4651.	3BR 2 BA, big apt, d/w, cac, w/d, $1400 + util. Avail 9/15. 727-4981.
1 BR 1 BA, w/w, catv, nr hospital, $750 + util. Avail 10/1. 589-7315.	2 BR 1 1/2 BA, pkg, nr airport, d/w, incl catv, $875 + elec. 863-4193.

1. You're looking for a one-bedroom apartment. Which number will you call?
   - Ⓐ 273-4651.
   - Ⓑ 589-7315.
   - Ⓒ 727-4981.
   - Ⓓ 863-4193.

2. You need an apartment with two bathrooms. Which number will you call?
   - Ⓐ 863-4193.
   - Ⓑ 273-4651.
   - Ⓒ 589-7315.
   - Ⓓ 727-4981.

3. Which apartment includes utilities?
   - Ⓐ The 2-bedroom apartment with 1 bath.
   - Ⓑ The 2-bedroom apartment with 1 1/2 baths.
   - Ⓒ The 3-bedroom apartment.
   - Ⓓ The 1-bedroom apartment.

4. Which apartment doesn't have a dishwasher?
   - Ⓐ The 2-bedroom apartment with 1 bath.
   - Ⓑ The 2-bedroom apartment with 1 1/2 baths.
   - Ⓒ The 1-bedroom apartment.
   - Ⓓ The 3-bedroom apartment.

5. Which apartment is available on Sept. 15?
   - Ⓐ The 2-bedroom apartment with 1 bath.
   - Ⓑ The 2-bedroom apartment with 1 1/2 baths.
   - Ⓒ The 1-bedroom apartment.
   - Ⓓ The 3-bedroom apartment.

6. How many of these apartments have cable TV?
   - Ⓐ One.
   - Ⓑ Two.
   - Ⓒ Three.
   - Ⓓ Four.

7. How much is the rent for the apartment near the hospital?
   - Ⓐ $750 plus utilities.
   - Ⓑ $875 plus electricity.
   - Ⓒ $950 plus utilities.
   - Ⓓ $1400 plus utilities.

8. What does the 3-bedroom apartment have that the other apartments don't have?
   - Ⓐ Two bathrooms and a dishwasher.
   - Ⓑ A dishwasher and central air conditioning.
   - Ⓒ A dishwasher and a washer and dryer.
   - Ⓓ A washer and dryer and central air conditioning.

9. You're a pilot. You and a friend are looking for an apartment. Which number will you call?
   - Ⓐ 863-4193.
   - Ⓑ 727-4981.
   - Ⓒ 273-4651.
   - Ⓓ 589-7315.

10. What does the 1-bedroom apartment have that the other apartments don't have?
   - Ⓐ Cable TV.
   - Ⓑ Wall-to-wall carpeting.
   - Ⓒ A dishwasher.
   - Ⓓ A washer and dryer.

1 Ⓐ Ⓑ Ⓒ Ⓓ   4 Ⓐ Ⓑ Ⓒ Ⓓ   7 Ⓐ Ⓑ Ⓒ Ⓓ   10 Ⓐ Ⓑ Ⓒ Ⓓ

2 Ⓐ Ⓑ Ⓒ Ⓓ   5 Ⓐ Ⓑ Ⓒ Ⓓ   8 Ⓐ Ⓑ Ⓒ Ⓓ

3 Ⓐ Ⓑ Ⓒ Ⓓ   6 Ⓐ Ⓑ Ⓒ Ⓓ   9 Ⓐ Ⓑ Ⓒ Ⓓ

Choose the correct answer to complete the conversation.

11. Is the apartment furnished _____ unfurnished?
   Ⓐ and
   Ⓑ but
   Ⓒ or
   Ⓓ with

12. It's unfurnished. _____ any furniture in the unit.
   Ⓐ Isn't
   Ⓑ There isn't
   Ⓒ Aren't
   Ⓓ There aren't

13. Is there public _____ nearby?
   Ⓐ communication
   Ⓑ location
   Ⓒ station
   Ⓓ transportation

14. Yes. There's a bus stop _____ the corner.
   Ⓐ around
   Ⓑ between
   Ⓒ next
   Ⓓ across

15. _____ is the rent?
   Ⓐ How many
   Ⓑ What does it cost
   Ⓒ How much
   Ⓓ What is the price

16. _____
   Ⓐ On the third floor.
   Ⓑ On the first day of the month.
   Ⓒ Every month.
   Ⓓ $800 a month.

17. _____ a security deposit?
   Ⓐ Are you
   Ⓑ Is there
   Ⓒ Am I
   Ⓓ Is it

18. Yes. We require one month rent in advance when you _____ the lease.
   Ⓐ sign
   Ⓑ print
   Ⓒ leave
   Ⓓ signature

19. Is the building in _____ neighborhood?
   Ⓐ a dangerous
   Ⓑ an empty
   Ⓒ an inconvenient
   Ⓓ a convenient

20. Yes. _____ many stores in the neighborhood, and _____ a school nearby.
   Ⓐ There is . . . there's
   Ⓑ There is . . . there are
   Ⓒ There are . . . there's
   Ⓓ There are . . . there are

21. Are pets _____?
   Ⓐ loud
   Ⓑ allowed
   Ⓒ may they
   Ⓓ can we

22. Yes. Dogs and cats _____.
   Ⓐ have permission
   Ⓑ is permitted
   Ⓒ are permitted
   Ⓓ are you allowed

11 Ⓐ Ⓑ Ⓒ Ⓓ   14 Ⓐ Ⓑ Ⓒ Ⓓ   17 Ⓐ Ⓑ Ⓒ Ⓓ   20 Ⓐ Ⓑ Ⓒ Ⓓ

12 Ⓐ Ⓑ Ⓒ Ⓓ   15 Ⓐ Ⓑ Ⓒ Ⓓ   18 Ⓐ Ⓑ Ⓒ Ⓓ   21 Ⓐ Ⓑ Ⓒ Ⓓ

13 Ⓐ Ⓑ Ⓒ Ⓓ   16 Ⓐ Ⓑ Ⓒ Ⓓ   19 Ⓐ Ⓑ Ⓒ Ⓓ   22 Ⓐ Ⓑ Ⓒ Ⓓ

Go to the next page ⟶

C GRAMMAR IN CONTEXT: Describing Maintenance & Repairs Needed in a Rental Unit

23. Hello. This is David Lee, the new tenant in Apartment 412. There are _____ in my apartment.
- Ⓐ broken
- Ⓑ a problem
- Ⓒ many repairs
- Ⓓ many problems

24. What's the _____ ?
- Ⓐ matter
- Ⓑ repair
- Ⓒ problems
- Ⓓ troubles

25. The doorbell is broken. _____
- Ⓐ It doesn't open.
- Ⓑ It doesn't lock.
- Ⓒ It doesn't ring.
- Ⓓ It doesn't close.

26. _____ And what else?
- Ⓐ You see.
- Ⓑ I see.
- Ⓒ It sees.
- Ⓓ We see.

I understand.

27. The oven doesn't light. _____
- Ⓐ The kitchen is dark.
- Ⓑ I can't bake.
- Ⓒ I can't see inside the oven.
- Ⓓ My food always burns.

28. The bathtub is cracked. _____
- Ⓐ There's water on the bathroom floor.
- Ⓑ The roof is leaking.
- Ⓒ The sink is leaking.
- Ⓓ There's water on the kitchen floor.

29. Okay. _____
- Ⓐ Else?
- Ⓑ Other?
- Ⓒ Anything?
- Ⓓ Anything else?

30. Yes. One more thing. The kitchen sink is clogged. _____
- Ⓐ The water is too hot.
- Ⓑ The water is too cold.
- Ⓒ The water doesn't go down the drain.
- Ⓓ Water doesn't come out of the faucet.

31. All right. I'll send someone to _____ everything right away.
- Ⓐ repair
- Ⓑ break
- Ⓒ fixes
- Ⓓ will fix

32. You're welcome, and I _____ for the inconvenience.
- Ⓐ please
- Ⓑ thank you
- Ⓒ sorry
- Ⓓ apologize

Thank you very much.

23 Ⓐ Ⓑ Ⓒ Ⓓ 26 Ⓐ Ⓑ Ⓒ Ⓓ 29 Ⓐ Ⓑ Ⓒ Ⓓ 32 Ⓐ Ⓑ Ⓒ Ⓓ

24 Ⓐ Ⓑ Ⓒ Ⓓ 27 Ⓐ Ⓑ Ⓒ Ⓓ 30 Ⓐ Ⓑ Ⓒ Ⓓ

25 Ⓐ Ⓑ Ⓒ Ⓓ 28 Ⓐ Ⓑ Ⓒ Ⓓ 31 Ⓐ Ⓑ Ⓒ Ⓓ

D READING: A Floor Plan

Look at the floor plan for this apartment. Choose the correct answer.

33. How many bedrooms are there?
   - Ⓐ One.
   - Ⓑ Two.
   - Ⓒ Three.
   - Ⓓ Four.

34. How many closets are there?
   - Ⓐ One.
   - Ⓑ Two.
   - Ⓒ Three.
   - Ⓓ Four.

35. How many bathrooms are there?
   - Ⓐ One.
   - Ⓑ Two.
   - Ⓒ Three.
   - Ⓓ Four.

36. How many bathtubs are there?
   - Ⓐ One.
   - Ⓑ Two.
   - Ⓒ Three.
   - Ⓓ Four.

E LISTENING ASSESSMENT: Inquiring About a Rental Unit

Read and listen to the questions. Then listen to the conversation and answer the questions.

37. Where is the 1-bedroom apartment?
   - Ⓐ On the first floor.
   - Ⓑ On the second floor.
   - Ⓒ On the fifth floor.
   - Ⓓ On the sixth floor.

38. How much is the rent on the 2-bedroom unit?
   - Ⓐ $800 a month.
   - Ⓑ $800 a week.
   - Ⓒ $1,100 a year.
   - Ⓓ $1,100 a month.

39. Which pets are allowed in the building?
   - Ⓐ Dogs, cats, and smaller pets.
   - Ⓑ Cats and smaller pets.
   - Ⓒ Cats only.
   - Ⓓ Dogs only.

40. How much is the security deposit on the 1-bedroom apartment?
   - Ⓐ $800
   - Ⓑ $1,100
   - Ⓒ $1,600
   - Ⓓ $2,200

F WRITING ASSESSMENT

Describe your apartment or home.
Write about the rooms, the building, and the neighborhood.
(Use a separate sheet of paper.)

G SPEAKING ASSESSMENT

I can ask and answer these questions:

Ask Answer

☐ ☐ How many rooms are there in your apartment or home? Describe them.
☐ ☐ What's your favorite room? Why?
☐ ☐ Tell me about your neighborhood.

33 Ⓐ Ⓑ Ⓒ Ⓓ   35 Ⓐ Ⓑ Ⓒ Ⓓ   37 Ⓐ Ⓑ Ⓒ Ⓓ   39 Ⓐ Ⓑ Ⓒ Ⓓ
34 Ⓐ Ⓑ Ⓒ Ⓓ   36 Ⓐ Ⓑ Ⓒ Ⓓ   38 Ⓐ Ⓑ Ⓒ Ⓓ   40 Ⓐ Ⓑ Ⓒ Ⓓ   STOP

Name _____

Date _____ **Class** _____

A IDENTIFYING PARTS OF THE FACE & BODY

Choose the correct answer.

Example:

ⓐ arm
ⓑ foot
● hand
ⓓ toe

1. ⓐ ears
   ⓑ fingers
   ⓒ toes
   ⓓ lips

2. ⓐ wrist
   ⓑ ankle
   ⓒ elbow
   ⓓ arm

3. ⓐ beard
   ⓑ mustache
   ⓒ eyebrow
   ⓓ eyelash

4. ⓐ wrist
   ⓑ shoulder
   ⓒ ankle
   ⓓ elbow

5. ⓐ hip
   ⓑ leg
   ⓒ shoulder
   ⓓ thigh

B COMMON SYMPTOMS

Choose the correct answer.

6. My temperature is 102° F. I have _____.
   ⓐ a sweater
   ⓑ an oven
   ⓒ high blood pressure
   ⓓ a fever

7. Timmy needs a tissue. He has _____.
   ⓐ a runny nose
   ⓑ a sore throat
   ⓒ a backache
   ⓓ a fever

8. Carla ate too much candy. Now she has _____.
   ⓐ an earache
   ⓑ a toothache
   ⓒ a cold
   ⓓ a runny nose

9. That music was loud! I have _____.
   ⓐ a stiff back
   ⓑ a cold
   ⓒ a head
   ⓓ an earache

10. I sang all day. Now I have _____.
    ⓐ a backache
    ⓑ an earache
    ⓒ a sore throat
    ⓓ a sprained ankle

11. I think I have a cold. I have a bad _____.
    ⓐ sneeze
    ⓑ cough
    ⓒ throat
    ⓓ nose

1 ⓐ ⓑ ⓒ ⓓ   4 ⓐ ⓑ ⓒ ⓓ   7 ⓐ ⓑ ⓒ ⓓ   10 ⓐ ⓑ ⓒ ⓓ

2 ⓐ ⓑ ⓒ ⓓ   5 ⓐ ⓑ ⓒ ⓓ   8 ⓐ ⓑ ⓒ ⓓ   11 ⓐ ⓑ ⓒ ⓓ

3 ⓐ ⓑ ⓒ ⓓ   6 ⓐ ⓑ ⓒ ⓓ   9 ⓐ ⓑ ⓒ ⓓ

Go to the next page   **T47**

C GRAMMAR IN CONTEXT: Calling to Report an Absence; Making a Doctor Appointment

Choose the correct answer to complete the conversations.

Woodlawn Elementary School.

12. Hello. This is Amy Long. My son, Paul, _____ absent today because _____ sick.
- Ⓐ will . . . he's
- Ⓑ will be . . . he's
- Ⓒ won't be . . . he
- Ⓓ can't . . . he

13. _____ class is he in?
- Ⓐ Which
- Ⓑ Who
- Ⓒ Where
- Ⓓ When

He's in Mr. Wilson's 4th grade class.

Doctor's office.

14. Hello. This is Alicia Flores. I don't _____ well.
- Ⓐ sick
- Ⓒ feel
- Ⓑ healthy
- Ⓓ feeling

15. _____ the matter?
- Ⓐ How's
- Ⓑ Why's
- Ⓒ Where's
- Ⓓ What's

I have a very bad stomachache.

16. Do you want to make _____?
- Ⓐ medicine
- Ⓑ see the doctor
- Ⓒ a reservation
- Ⓓ an appointment

Yes, please.

17. _____ tomorrow at 2 PM?
- Ⓐ Can you come in
- Ⓑ Can you go
- Ⓒ Are you sick
- Ⓓ Is the doctor here

2 PM? Yes. Thank you.

D PROCEDURES DURING A MEDICAL EXAM

18. The nurse took my blood _____.
- Ⓐ pulse
- Ⓒ pressure
- Ⓑ weight
- Ⓓ temperature

20. He measured my _____ on the scale.
- Ⓐ wait
- Ⓒ weight
- Ⓑ waist
- Ⓓ pulse

19. The doctor listened to my heart with _____.
- Ⓐ a scale
- Ⓒ an X-ray
- Ⓑ a stethoscope
- Ⓓ a headphone

21. She _____ my eyes, ears, nose, and throat.
- Ⓐ took
- Ⓒ measured
- Ⓑ listened to
- Ⓓ examined

. . . .

12 Ⓐ Ⓑ Ⓒ Ⓓ   15 Ⓐ Ⓑ Ⓒ Ⓓ   18 Ⓐ Ⓑ Ⓒ Ⓓ   21 Ⓐ Ⓑ Ⓒ Ⓓ

13 Ⓐ Ⓑ Ⓒ Ⓓ   16 Ⓐ Ⓑ Ⓒ Ⓓ   19 Ⓐ Ⓑ Ⓒ Ⓓ

14 Ⓐ Ⓑ Ⓒ Ⓓ   17 Ⓐ Ⓑ Ⓒ Ⓓ   20 Ⓐ Ⓑ Ⓒ Ⓓ   **Go to the next page** ⟹

Name _____ **Date** _____

E COMMON PRESCRIPTION & NON-PRESCRIPTION MEDICATIONS

22. The doctor recommended _____ for the rash on my arm.
- (A) anti-itch cream
- (B) throat lozenges
- (C) cough syrup
- (D) antacid tablets

23. I'm taking _____ for my upset stomach.
- (A) cough syrup
- (B) antacid tablets
- (C) throat lozenges
- (D) aspirin

24. The doctor gave me a prescription for _____ for my throat infection.
- (A) vitamins
- (B) cold medicine
- (C) ear drops
- (D) penicillin

25. I sneeze and cough every spring, so the clinic gives me a prescription for _____.
- (A) throat lozenges
- (B) cough syrup
- (C) allergy medication
- (D) cold medicine

F READING: Medicine Label Dosages

Choose the correct medicine label for each instruction.

CLR 4 tabs. 2x/day Rx	Lincoln Pharmacy 2 tsps. 2x/day Rx	Olympic Pharmacies 2 caps. 2x/day Rx	MacLeod Drugs 2 pills 4x/day
A	**B**	**C**	**D**

26. Take two pills four times a day.
(A) (B) (C) (D)

27. Take two teaspoons two times a day.
(A) (B) (C) (D)

28. Twice a day take four tablets.
(A) (B) (C) (D)

29. Take two capsules twice a day.
(A) (B) (C) (D)

G READING: Medicine Label Instructions

Brookdale Pharmacy Rx For external use only	Park Pharmacy Take medication on an empty stomach. Rx	J&M Rx Avoid dairy products and chocolate while taking this medicine.	Sunrise Pharmacy Rx IMPORTANT. Finish all this medication
A	**B**	**C**	**D**

30. Do not drink milk or other milk products.
(A) (B) (C) (D)

31. Do not eat or drink this medicine.
(A) (B) (C) (D)

32. Take 1 hour before or 2-3 hours after you eat.
(A) (B) (C) (D)

33. Even if you feel better, don't stop taking this medicine.
(A) (B) (C) (D)

....

22 (A) (B) (C) (D)   25 (A) (B) (C) (D)   28 (A) (B) (C) (D)   31 (A) (B) (C) (D)
23 (A) (B) (C) (D)   26 (A) (B) (C) (D)   29 (A) (B) (C) (D)   32 (A) (B) (C) (D)
24 (A) (B) (C) (D)   27 (A) (B) (C) (D)   30 (A) (B) (C) (D)   33 (A) (B) (C) (D)

H CLOZE READING: A Note to the Teacher

Deer   Dare   Dear   Mr. Harper,
ⓐ   ⓑ   ●

My daughter, Jenny, was   present   absent   not ³⁴ from school yesterday
                            ⓐ   ⓑ   ⓒ

reason   because   for ³⁵ she had a very   full   good   bad ³⁶ stomachache and I took
ⓐ   ⓑ   ⓒ   ⓐ   ⓑ   ⓒ

her   him   it ³⁷ to the doctor.
ⓐ   ⓑ   ⓒ

Sincerely,

Barbara Taylor

I LISTENING ASSESSMENT: Making a Doctor Appointment

Read and listen to the questions. Then listen to the conversation and answer the questions.

38. When did she hurt her back?
    ⓐ Today.
    ⓑ Yesterday.
    ⓒ Last Tuesday.
    ⓓ Last Thursday.

39. Where did she hurt it?
    ⓐ At home.
    ⓑ At the clinic.
    ⓒ On the telephone.
    ⓓ On the job.

40. What time does she have to be at the clinic?
    ⓐ 7:15 AM.
    ⓑ 7:30 AM.
    ⓒ 7:45 AM.
    ⓓ 7:30 PM.

J WRITING ASSESSMENT: Fill Out the Medical History Form

MEDICAL HISTORY

Name _____   Date of Birth ____ / ____ / ____
    First   M. I.   Last   Month Day Year

Address _____
    Number Street   City   State   Zip Code

Telephone: Home _____ Work _____ Height _____ Weight _____

Emergency Contact: Name _____ Relationship _____ Telephone _____

Do you have:	YES	NO		YES	NO		YES	NO
heart disease?	☐	☐	allergies?	☐	☐	other problems?	☐	☐
kidney disease?	☐	☐	headaches?	☐	☐	Do you smoke?	☐	☐
high blood pressure?	☐	☐	trouble sleeping?	☐	☐	Do you drink?	☐	☐
diabetes?	☐	☐	trouble eating?	☐	☐	Are you taking medicine now?	☐	☐

If you answered Yes above, explain: _____

_____

K SPEAKING ASSESSMENT

I can ask and answer these questions:

Ask Answer
☐ ☐ How do you feel?
☐ ☐ When was your last appointment at
     a clinic or doctor's office?

Ask Answer
☐ ☐ Are you taking any medicine now?
☐ ☐ Is there any history of medical problems
     in your family? Explain.

Name _____

Date _____ Class _____

12

A FAHRENHEIT & CELSIUS TEMPERATURES

Look at the thermometer. Choose the correct temperature.

1. 84° F.
   - Ⓐ 0° C.
   - Ⓑ 12° C.
   - Ⓒ 29° C.
   - Ⓓ 84° C.

2. 32° F.
   - Ⓐ -32° C.
   - Ⓑ 0° C.
   - Ⓒ 32° C.
   - Ⓓ 64° C.

3. -16° C.
   - Ⓐ 9° F.
   - Ⓑ 61° F.
   - Ⓒ -16° F.
   - Ⓓ -9° F.

4. 12° C.
   - Ⓐ -12° F.
   - Ⓑ 17° F.
   - Ⓒ 53° F.
   - Ⓓ 70° F.

B TEMPERATURE VALUES

Choose the correct temperature.

5. It's very hot today. It's _____.
   - Ⓐ 35° C.
   - Ⓑ 35° F.

6. It's very cold today. It's _____.
   - Ⓐ 28° C.
   - Ⓑ 15° F.

7. I have a fever. My temperature is _____.
   - Ⓐ 39° F.
   - Ⓑ 39° C.

8. The water is beginning to freeze. It's _____.
   - Ⓐ 0° C.
   - Ⓑ 0° F.

9. The cake is baking in the oven at _____.
   - Ⓐ 350° C.
   - Ⓑ 350° F.

10. The water is starting to boil. Its temperature is _____.
    - Ⓐ 100° C.
    - Ⓑ 100° F.

°F   °C

1 Ⓐ Ⓑ Ⓒ Ⓓ   4 Ⓐ Ⓑ Ⓒ Ⓓ   7 Ⓐ Ⓑ Ⓒ Ⓓ   10 Ⓐ Ⓑ Ⓒ Ⓓ

2 Ⓐ Ⓑ Ⓒ Ⓓ   5 Ⓐ Ⓑ Ⓒ Ⓓ   8 Ⓐ Ⓑ Ⓒ Ⓓ

3 Ⓐ Ⓑ Ⓒ Ⓓ   6 Ⓐ Ⓑ Ⓒ Ⓓ   9 Ⓐ Ⓑ Ⓒ Ⓓ   Go to the next page >   **T51**

C GRAMMAR IN CONTEXT: Beginning & Ending a Telephone Conversation

Example:

Hello. This is Robert Simon.
_____ to Ms. Harris?

- Ⓐ Can I
- Ⓑ Is she there
- Ⓒ May you speak
- ⬤ May I speak

Thank you.

11. Just _____. Let me see if she's here.
- Ⓐ today
- Ⓑ an hour
- Ⓒ you wait
- Ⓓ a moment

12. I'm sorry. She isn't here right now. Can I _____?
- Ⓐ give a message
- Ⓑ give you a message
- Ⓒ take a message
- Ⓓ leave you a message

13. Yes. Please tell _____ that Robert Simon called.
- Ⓐ she
- Ⓑ me
- Ⓒ you
- Ⓓ her

14. All right. I'll _____.
- Ⓐ give the message
- Ⓑ give her the message
- Ⓒ give you the message
- Ⓓ give me the message

D READING: Telephone Directory White Pages

Look at the telephone listings. Choose the correct answer.

15. What is John Gavin Singleton's phone number?
- Ⓐ 815 267-9534
- Ⓒ 815 495-8197
- Ⓑ 719 389-7283
- Ⓓ 815 459-8197

16. What is Rajdeep Singh's telephone number?
- Ⓐ 719 387-2415
- Ⓒ 815 426-3317
- Ⓑ 815 637-2148
- Ⓓ 815 387-2415

17. What street does Brenda Singer live on?
- Ⓐ Main Street.
- Ⓒ Center Street.
- Ⓑ Lake Street.
- Ⓓ Central Avenue.

18. What town does Linda live in?
- Ⓐ Wellington.
- Ⓒ Willston.
- Ⓑ Holbrook.
- Ⓓ Hopedale.

19. What town does Dennis Singleton live in?
- Ⓐ Arlington.
- Ⓒ Willston.
- Ⓑ Wellington.
- Ⓓ Holbrook.

SINCLAIR—SINGLETON	649
SINGER Alexander 42 Lake Nor 815 427-7251	
Dennis 143 Main Arl 815 639-9148	
Tom & Brenda 1423 Central Wil 719 825-1491	
SINGH Hardeep 753 Pond Arl 815 637-2148	
Madan 2213 River Nor 815 426-3317	
R 1719 School Hol 719 387-2415	
SINGLER Linda 27 Oak Wil 719 828-4124	
SINGLETON D 819 Shore Wel 815 267-9534	
John E 238 Maple Hol 719 389-7283	
John G 12 Adams Hop 815 495-8197	

RESIDENCE LISTING

11	Ⓐ Ⓑ Ⓒ Ⓓ	14	Ⓐ Ⓑ Ⓒ Ⓓ	17	Ⓐ Ⓑ Ⓒ Ⓓ
12	Ⓐ Ⓑ Ⓒ Ⓓ	15	Ⓐ Ⓑ Ⓒ Ⓓ	18	Ⓐ Ⓑ Ⓒ Ⓓ
13	Ⓐ Ⓑ Ⓒ Ⓓ	16	Ⓐ Ⓑ Ⓒ Ⓓ	19	Ⓐ Ⓑ Ⓒ Ⓓ

Go to the next page

Name _____ **Date** _____

NORTHBORO TOWN OF

AMBULANCE	
Emergency Only	911
ANIMAL CONTROL	815 821-6014
BOARD OF HEALTH	815 821-6020
ELECTRIC LIGHT DEPT	815 821-6035
HIGHWAY DEPT	815 821-6040
LIBRARY 400 Main Nor	815 821-6030
PARKS & RECREATION	815 821-6018
POLICE—	
Emergency Only	911
All Other Purposes	815 821-5000
SCHOOLS—	
Elementary—	
Eastwick 360 Main Nor	815 821-6130
Middle School—	
Jefferson 120 Central Nor	815 821-6140
High School–	
Lincoln 72 School Nor	815 821-6180

Pizza

Classic Pizza & Pasta
124 Main Ple...........................315 469-7750
Jimmy's House of Pizza
32 Western Ree.....................315 727-9123

Plants—Retail

Flowers For You
1200 Central Ree....................315 727-4124

Plumbing Contractors

AJAX Plumbing
See Our Display Ad Page 307
1450 Central Ree....................315 729-4000
DUFFY & SONS
632 Lake Wat...........................418 274-1234
Landry Plumbing & Heating
27 Pine Wal.............................418 829-3600
Reliable Plumbing
4250 Lawson Wol.....................315 643-2121

20. The street lamp on Hernan's street is broken. What number should he call?
   Ⓐ 911
   Ⓑ 815 821-5000
   Ⓒ 815 821-6014
   Ⓓ 815 821-6035

21. A very mean dog is running up and down the street in front of Claudia's apartment building. What number should she call?
   Ⓐ 815 821-6020
   Ⓑ 815 821-6018
   Ⓒ 815 821-6040
   Ⓓ 815 821-6014

22. The Chungs just moved to Northboro. They want to enroll their son in 10th grade. What number should they call?
   Ⓐ 815 821-6160
   Ⓑ 815 621-6140
   Ⓒ 815 821-6130
   Ⓓ 815 821-6060

23. The Hills ate at a restaurant yesterday. This morning they all have terrible stomachaches. They think the chicken at the restaurant was bad. What number should they call?
   Ⓐ 815 821-6014
   Ⓑ 815 821-6030
   Ⓒ 815 821-6020
   Ⓓ 815 821-5000

24. There's broken glass in the playground across the street from the police station. What number should you call?
   Ⓐ 815 821-6130
   Ⓑ 815 821-6018
   Ⓒ 815 821-5000
   Ⓓ 911

25. What is the phone number of the pizza shop in Pleasantville?
   Ⓐ 315 727-9123
   Ⓑ 315 469-7750
   Ⓒ 315 727-9213
   Ⓓ 315 469-7550

26. Which town in this area has a place to buy plants and flowers?
   Ⓐ Retail
   Ⓑ Centerville
   Ⓒ Remington
   Ⓓ Reedsville

27. What's the telephone number of the plumbing company in Watertown?
   Ⓐ 315 729-4000
   Ⓑ 418 829-3600
   Ⓒ 418 274-1234
   Ⓓ 315 643-2121

28. Where is the Ajax Plumbing Company located?
   Ⓐ On page 307.
   Ⓑ In Remington.
   Ⓒ On Central Ave.
   Ⓓ 315 729-4000.

29. You live in Wallingford, and you need a plumber right away! What number should you call for the closest plumber?
   Ⓐ 315 643-2121
   Ⓑ 418 829-3600
   Ⓒ 418 274-1234
   Ⓓ 315 729-4000

20 Ⓐ Ⓑ Ⓒ Ⓓ   23 Ⓐ Ⓑ Ⓒ Ⓓ   26 Ⓐ Ⓑ Ⓒ Ⓓ   29 Ⓐ Ⓑ Ⓒ Ⓓ

21 Ⓐ Ⓑ Ⓒ Ⓓ   24 Ⓐ Ⓑ Ⓒ Ⓓ   27 Ⓐ Ⓑ Ⓒ Ⓓ

22 Ⓐ Ⓑ Ⓒ Ⓓ   25 Ⓐ Ⓑ Ⓒ Ⓓ   28 Ⓐ Ⓑ Ⓒ Ⓓ

Go to the next page ➤ **T53**

F CLOZE READING: Phone Messages

Choose the correct answers to complete the messages.

Mom [call (A)] [calls (B)] [called ●] at 4:00. She [has (A)] [have (B)] [having (C)] ³⁰ to work late at the

office this evening. [She (A)] [She'll (B)] [She's (C)] ³¹ be home at about 9 PM.

Mr. Slate called [to (A)] [from (B)] [through (C)] ³² the garage about your car repairs. You should call

[us (A)] [her (B)] [him (C)] ³³ as soon as possible.

Grandma and Grandpa called to [speak (A)] [tell (B)] [say (C)] ³⁴ hello. [We're (A)] [They're (B)] [You're (C)] ³⁵

fine, and you don't have to call [them (A)] [they (B)] [their (C)] ³⁶ back.

G LISTENING ASSESSMENT: Recorded Telephone Information

Read and listen to the questions. Then listen to the library's recorded announcements and answer the questions.

37. When does the book club meet?
    - Ⓐ On the 1st Tuesday of each month.
    - Ⓑ On the 3rd Tuesday of each month.
    - Ⓒ On the 1st Thursday of each month.
    - Ⓓ On the 3rd Thursday of each month.

38. How many evening programs are there each month?
    - Ⓐ One.
    - Ⓑ Two.
    - Ⓒ Three.
    - Ⓓ Four.

39. How many hours is the library open on Wednesdays?
    - Ⓐ 4 hours.
    - Ⓑ 6 hours.
    - Ⓒ 9 hours.
    - Ⓓ 12 hours.

40. On which date will the children's story hour meet?
    - Ⓐ March 5.
    - Ⓑ March 12.
    - Ⓒ March 19.
    - Ⓓ March 26.

H WRITING ASSESSMENT

Write about how you use the telephone. Do you use the telephone for work or for school? Do you talk to family members or friends in other places? Who do you talk to? How often? (Use a separate sheet of paper.)

I SPEAKING ASSESSMENT

I can call someone and answer the phone using these expressions:

Call Answer

☐ ☐ Hello. This is _____. May I please speak to _____?

☐ ☐ _____ isn't here right now. Can I take a message?

☐ ☐ Yes. Please tell _____ that _____.

---

30 Ⓐ Ⓑ Ⓒ Ⓓ   33 Ⓐ Ⓑ Ⓒ Ⓓ   36 Ⓐ Ⓑ Ⓒ Ⓓ   39 Ⓐ Ⓑ Ⓒ Ⓓ

31 Ⓐ Ⓑ Ⓒ Ⓓ   34 Ⓐ Ⓑ Ⓒ Ⓓ   37 Ⓐ Ⓑ Ⓒ Ⓓ   40 Ⓐ Ⓑ Ⓒ Ⓓ

32 Ⓐ Ⓑ Ⓒ Ⓓ   35 Ⓐ Ⓑ Ⓒ Ⓓ   38 Ⓐ Ⓑ Ⓒ Ⓓ

STOP

A HOUSEHOLD REPAIR PROBLEMS

Choose the correct answer to complete the conversation.

1. My washing machine is broken.
   You should call _____.
   - Ⓐ a TV repairperson
   - Ⓑ an appliance repairperson
   - Ⓒ an electrician
   - Ⓓ a plumber

2. Somebody stole the keys to my apartment.
   You should call _____.
   - Ⓐ a carpenter
   - Ⓑ a plumber
   - Ⓒ a painter
   - Ⓓ a locksmith

3. Smoke comes into the room when we use the fireplace.
   You should call _____.
   - Ⓐ a chimneysweep
   - Ⓑ the fire department
   - Ⓒ a carpenter
   - Ⓓ a painter

4. Channels 2 through 50 are okay, but Channels 51 through 100 have a very bad picture.
   We should call _____.
   - Ⓐ an electrician
   - Ⓑ an appliance repairperson
   - Ⓒ a TV repairperson
   - Ⓓ the cable TV company

5. Look at all these bugs!
   We should call _____.
   - Ⓐ an electrician
   - Ⓑ the animal control officer
   - Ⓒ an exterminator
   - Ⓓ the zoo

6. I couldn't fix the doorbell.
   Let's call _____.
   - Ⓐ a locksmith
   - Ⓑ an electrician
   - Ⓒ an appliance repairperson
   - Ⓓ a mechanic

B GRAMMAR IN CONTEXT: Securing Household Repair Services

Choose the correct answer to complete the conversation.

7. There's _____ wrong with my bathroom sink. Can you send _____ to fix it?
   - Ⓐ anything . . . anyone
   - Ⓑ anyone . . . anything
   - Ⓒ something . . . someone
   - Ⓓ someone . . . something

8. I can't send _____ today. Will _____ be home tomorrow at 10 AM?
   - Ⓐ somebody . . . somebody
   - Ⓑ anybody . . . anything
   - Ⓒ anybody . . . somebody
   - Ⓓ anything . . . something

9. I _____ be home at ten, but _____ be back at eleven. Is 11:00 okay?
   - Ⓐ won't . . . I'll
   - Ⓑ won't . . . you'll
   - Ⓒ will . . . I'll
   - Ⓓ will . . . you'll

10. Yes. _____ will be there at eleven.
   - Ⓐ Anything
   - Ⓑ Anybody
   - Ⓒ Something
   - Ⓓ Someone

C READING: A TV Schedule

Look at the TV listings. Choose the correct answer.

	6:00	6:30	7:00	7:30	8:00	8:30	9:00	9:30	10:00	10:30
2	News at 6 (News)	CBS Evening News (News)	Entertainment Tonight (Talk/Tabloid)	Who Wants to be a Millionaire (Game)	Life with Bobby: *Out to Lunch* (Comedy)	Everybody Loves Richard: *The Love Letter* (Comedy)	FBI Special Investigations Unit: *The Dangerous Package* (Crime)		PrimeTime Monday (Talk/Tabloid)	
4	Channel 4 News (News)	NBC Nightly News (News)	EXTRA (Talk/Tabloid)	Access Hollywood (Talk/Tabloid)	Happiest Class: *A New Teacher* (Comedy)	Wanda: *A Visitor from the Past* (Comedy)	Fletcher: *Bob's New Diet* (Comedy)	Fletcher: *Eat Your Vegetables* (Comedy)	Law & Order: *Bad Day at the Bank* (Crime)	
5	Everybody Loves Richard: *The First Day* (Comedy)	Everybody Loves Richard: *A New Friend* (Comedy)	Walt & Grace: *The Argument* (Comedy)	Neighbors: *The Lost Dog* (Comedy)	Biltmore Boys: *Alan's Problem* (Drama)		Three Sisters: *Trisha's New Boss* (Drama)		News at Ten (News)	
7	Eyewitness News (News)	ABC World News Tonight (News)	Jeopardy! (Game)	Wheel of Fortune (Game)	I'm With You: *Lost at the Mall* (Comedy)	Two by Two: *The School Dance* (Comedy)	According to Amy: *The Phone Message* (Comedy)	Better Than Ever: *Jim's New Couch* (Comedy)	LAPD Red: *Fight on the Freeway* (Crime)	
9	Baseball: *Anaheim Angels at Texas Rangers* (Sports) (Live)				KCAL 9 News at 8:00 PM		KCAL 9 News at 9:00 PM		KCAL 9 News at 10:00 PM (News)	Sports Central (News)
11	The Sampsons: *You're Fired!* (Cartoon)	Queen of the Hill: *Sally's New Car* (Comedy)	The Prince of Long Beach: *The Car Accident* (Comedy)	The Sampsons: *Henry's New Job* (Cartoon)	Downtown Medical Center: *Bad Day in the ER* (Reality)		Lost on an Island (Reality)		Fox 11 Ten O'Clock News (News)	
22	Cuanto Cuesta el Show (Game)	Noticias 22 (News)		El Tribunal del Pueblo (Reality)	El Hijo de Pedro Navajas (1986, Spanish)				Noticias 22 (News)	Contacto Deportivo (Sports/Info)
28	The NewsHour (News/Talk)	California's Golden Parks (Nature)		In the Kitchen (Cooking)	This Old Apartment: *Chicago* (Home Repair)		Great Performances: *Boston Symphony Orchestra in Moscow* (Concert)		NOVA: *Bugs, Bugs, Bugs* (Science)	

11. What's on Channel 5 at 7:00?
- Ⓐ *EXTRA.*
- Ⓑ *Walt & Grace.*
- Ⓒ *Jeopardy!*
- Ⓓ *Wheel of Fortune.*

12. What time is *Two by Two* on today?
- Ⓐ 8:00.
- Ⓑ 8:30.
- Ⓒ Channel 2.
- Ⓓ Channel 7.

13. What's on Channel 2 at 7:30?
- Ⓐ A game show.
- Ⓑ A comedy show.
- Ⓒ A news program.
- Ⓓ A cartoon program.

14. Which channel has programs in Spanish?
- Ⓐ Channel 5.
- Ⓑ Channel 11.
- Ⓒ Channel 22.
- Ⓓ Channel 28.

15. How many channels show the program *Everybody Loves Richard?*
- Ⓐ One.
- Ⓑ Two.
- Ⓒ Three.
- Ⓓ Four.

16. Which channels have news programs at 10:00?
- Ⓐ 2, 4, 7.
- Ⓑ 2, 4, 7, 28.
- Ⓒ 5, 9, 11.
- Ⓓ 5, 9, 11, 22.

17. My aunt loves classical music. What time is she going to watch TV today?
- Ⓐ 7:00.
- Ⓑ 8:00.
- Ⓒ 9:00.
- Ⓓ 10:00.

18. How many crime shows are on TV this evening?
- Ⓐ One.
- Ⓑ Two.
- Ⓒ Three.
- Ⓓ Four.

19. Which channel has the most news programs?
- Ⓐ Channel 2.
- Ⓑ Channel 4.
- Ⓒ Channel 7.
- Ⓓ Channel 9.

20. Which program isn't on tonight?
- Ⓐ *Neighbors.*
- Ⓑ *Friends.*
- Ⓒ *NOVA.*
- Ⓓ *LAPD Red.*

··

11 Ⓐ Ⓑ Ⓒ Ⓓ	14 Ⓐ Ⓑ Ⓒ Ⓓ	17 Ⓐ Ⓑ Ⓒ Ⓓ	20 Ⓐ Ⓑ Ⓒ Ⓓ
12 Ⓐ Ⓑ Ⓒ Ⓓ	15 Ⓐ Ⓑ Ⓒ Ⓓ	18 Ⓐ Ⓑ Ⓒ Ⓓ	
13 Ⓐ Ⓑ Ⓒ Ⓓ	16 Ⓐ Ⓑ Ⓒ Ⓓ	19 Ⓐ Ⓑ Ⓒ Ⓓ	

Go to the next page ⟩

D CLOZE READING: Household Repairs & Pronoun Review

Choose the correct answers to complete the story.

My brother is very upset. | She | He ● | We | is having a problem in | him | his | he | 21 apartment.
(A) (B) (C) — (A) (B) (C)

| He | Him | His | 22 oven is broken. | He | It | She | 23 doesn't go on. My brother tried to fix it
(A) (B) (C) — (A) (B) (C)

| itself | hisself | himself | 24, but he couldn't. He called the building manager a few days ago.
(A) (B) (C)

| She | Her | Hers | 25 wasn't there, so | it | she | he | 26 left a message on | she | her | hers | 27
(A) (B) (C) — (A) (B) (C) — (A) (B) (C)

answering machine. | He's | His | It's | 28 still waiting for | her | she | hers | 29 to call back. So while
(A) (B) (C) — (A) (B) (C)

my brother's oven is broken, | it | she | he | 30 comes over to | my | me | mine | 31 apartment and
(A) (B) (C) — (A) (B) (C)

uses | my | mine | me | 32. I'm happy to help | him | his | he | 33. After all, he's | me | my | mine | 34
(A) (B) (C) — (A) (B) (C) — (A) (B) (C)

brother!

E LISTENING ASSESSMENT: Recorded Telephone Instructions

Read and listen to the questions. Then listen to the telephone instructions and answer the questions.

35. Marina wants to fly from Los Angeles to Madrid, Spain. Which key should she press?
   (A) 1   (C) 3
   (B) 2   (D) 4

36. Roger wants to fly from Houston to Miami. Which key should he press?
   (A) 1   (C) 3
   (B) 2   (D) 4

37. Grace wants to make flight and hotel reservations for a tour of Italy. Which key should she press?
   (A) 1   (C) 3
   (B) 2   (D) 4

38. Daniel is looking for a job as a flight attendant. Which key should he press?
   (A) *   (C) 3
   (B) 1   (D) 5

39. Karen didn't hear the first two instructions. Which key should she press?
   (A) *   (C) 4
   (B) 1   (D) 5

40. Joseph is going to fly to New York tonight. Will his plane leave on time? Which key should he press?
   (A) *   (C) 2
   (B) 1   (D) 5

21 (A) (B) (C) (D)   27 (A) (B) (C) (D)   33 (A) (B) (C) (D)   39 (A) (B) (C) (D)

22 (A) (B) (C) (D)   28 (A) (B) (C) (D)   34 (A) (B) (C) (D)   40 (A) (B) (C) (D)

23 (A) (B) (C) (D)   29 (A) (B) (C) (D)   35 (A) (B) (C) (D)

24 (A) (B) (C) (D)   30 (A) (B) (C) (D)   36 (A) (B) (C) (D)

25 (A) (B) (C) (D)   31 (A) (B) (C) (D)   37 (A) (B) (C) (D)

26 (A) (B) (C) (D)   32 (A) (B) (C) (D)   38 (A) (B) (C) (D)

Go to the next page ⟩ T57 ●

F SKILL ASSESSMENT: Making a Schedule

Fill out the chart with your schedule for a typical week. Write in your times at school, at work, at meetings, and at other events. Also write in the things you do to relax, including sports, favorite TV shows, and other evening and weekend activities

	MON	TUE	WED	THU	FRI	SAT	SUN
6:00 AM							
7:00							
8:00							
9:00							
10:00							
11:00							
12:00 Noon							
1:00 PM							
2:00							
3:00							
4:00							
5:00							
6:00							
7:00							
8:00							
9:00							
10:00							
11:00							

G SPEAKING ASSESSMENT

I can ask and answer these questions:

Ask Answer

☐ ☐ When there's something wrong with an appliance in your apartment or home, who fixes it?

☐ ☐ Do you like to fix things?

☐ ☐ What can you fix?

Ask Answer

☐ ☐ Tell about your typical schedule during the week.

☐ ☐ Tell about your typical schedule on the weekend.

☐ ☐ What TV programs do you usually watch? When?

STOP

Listening Assessment Scripts

CHAPTER 1 TEST

Page T5, Section G

Read and listen to the questions.

38. What's his address?
39. When is his birthday?
40. How tall is he?

Now listen to the interview, and answer the questions.

A. What's your name?
B. Victor Sanchez.
A. What's your address?
B. 94 Center Street in Reedville.
A. And your telephone number?
B. (978) 583-4712.
A. What's your date of birth?
B. May thirteenth, nineteen eighty-three.
A. And what's your height?
B. I'm five feet eight inches tall.

CHAPTER 2 TEST

Page T10, Section G

Read and listen to the questions.

38. When DOESN'T the school have English classes?
39. Where is Wendy going to write her personal information?
40. At what time AREN'T there any classes at this school?

Now listen to the conversation, and answer the questions.

A. May I help you?
B. Yes. My name is Wendy Chen. I want to study English. Do you have English classes at this school?
A. Yes, we do. We have classes five days a week, Monday through Friday, in the morning and in the evening. Here's a registration form. Please print all your personal information in ink. Do you have a pen?
B. Yes, I do.
A. And do you have a document with your address?
B. Yes. I have a driver's license.
A. Good. Complete the form. Then give me the form and show me your driver's license. Then you're going to take a short English test.
B. Okay. Thank you.

CHAPTER 3 TEST

Page T14, Section H

Read and listen to the questions.

38. Where is the conversation taking place?
39. What is the customer going to have for an appetizer?
40. How many side orders is the customer going to have?

Now listen to the conversation, and answer the questions.

A. Are you ready to order?
B. Yes, I am. I'd like the baked chicken, please.
A. All right. And what side order are you going to have with that?
B. Let me have an order of rice and an order of carrots, please.
A. Do you want a salad with your meal?
B. No, I don't think so.
A. And do you want to start with an appetizer this evening?
B. Let me see. Yes. Please give me a bowl of vegetable soup.
A. Anything to drink?
B. Yes. A glass of milk, please.

CHAPTER 4 TEST

Page T18, Section E

Read and listen to the questions.

38. What day is it?
39. What are they going to do tomorrow?
40. Where are they going to meet?

Now listen to the conversation, and answer the questions.

A. Would you like to have dinner with me after work today?
B. I'm sorry. I can't. I go to a computer class every Tuesday after work.
A. How about tomorrow? Would you like to have dinner tomorrow?
B. Tomorrow? Yes. I'd love to.
A. Great. I'll meet you at five at your office. Okay?
B. Great.

CHAPTER 5 TEST

Page T22, Section E

Read and listen to the questions.

38. What do they disagree about?
39. What do they agree about?
40. Which opinion do they probably agree about?

Now listen to the conversation, and answer the questions.

A. You know, I think the streets in our city aren't as clean as they used to be.
B. I think so, too. But I think the buildings in our city are very interesting.
A. Do you really think so? In my opinion, the buildings in other cities around here are MORE interesting.
B. What do you think about the people in our city?
A. I think they're very friendly. Do you agree?
B. Definitely. And I think our parks are very beautiful.
A. I don't think so.

CHAPTER 6 TEST

Page T26, Section G

Read and listen to the questions.

38. How many items does the person want to return?
39. What's the matter with the shirt?
40. Where is the conversation taking place?

Now listen to the conversation, and answer the questions.

A. May I help you?
B. Yes, please. I want to return this shirt and this pair of pants.
A. What's the matter with them?
B. The shirt is too small, and the pants are too large.
A. I see. Do you want to exchange them?
B. No. I just want to return them, please.
A. All right. I'm afraid you can't return items here in the Men's Clothing department. You can return them at the Customer Service counter.
B. Where is that?
A. It's downstairs on the first floor next to the elevator.
B. Okay. Thanks very much.

CHAPTER 7 TEST

Page T32, Section H

Read and listen to the questions.

37. In which direction is the post office?
38. In which direction is the library?
39. In which direction is the shopping mall?
40. In which direction is the zoo?

Now listen to the conversation, and answer the questions.

A. Excuse me. I'm new here in town. Would you please tell me how to get to the post office from here?
B. Sure. Drive east along this street about three blocks and you'll see the post office on the right.
A. And could you please tell me how to get to the nearest shopping mall from here?
B. Yes. It's very easy. Turn left at the next street and then drive south for about two miles. The shopping mall is across from the airport.
A. Is there a library near here?
B. Yes. There's a brand new library about ten blocks from here. Just turn right and drive west along School Street, and you'll see the library across from the high school.
A. And can you recommend a place to go with my children?
B. Yes. We have a wonderful zoo.
A. Is it very far?
B. Not at all. It's about two miles north of here.
A. Well, thank you very much.
B. No problem. And welcome to Greenville!

CHAPTER 8 TEST

Page T38, Section H

Read and listen to the questions.

38. What kind of position is the person applying for?
39. Where is the conversation taking place?
40. How many years of work experience does the applicant have?

Now listen to the conversation, and answer the questions.

A. Tell me about your skills.
B. I can type, and I can file.
A. Do you know how to use accounting software on a computer?
B. Yes. I used accounting software in my previous job.
A. Where was that?

B. I worked at the Johnson Insurance Company.
A. How long did you work there?
B. For three years.
A. And where did you work before that?
B. I worked at the Larsen Real Estate agency for two years, and before that I worked as a cashier at the Citywide Supermarket for one year.
A. And why are you interested in a position with us at Landmark Data Management?
B. I know this is an excellent company, and I think that I can be a very effective and useful employee here.

CHAPTER 9 TEST

Page T42, Section G

Read and listen to the questions.

38. When did the person fall?
39. What's their address?
40. Where is their apartment?

Now listen to the conversation, and answer the questions.

A. Emergency Operator.
B. I want to report an emergency.
A. Yes. Go ahead.
B. My mother tripped and fell while she was walking down the stairs in our building. She can't speak to me.
A. What's your address?
B. 30 East Street in Westville.
A. Is that an apartment building or a home?
B. An apartment building. We're on the sixth floor in Apartment 6-D.
A. Okay. Stay with your mother but don't move her. An ambulance is on the way.
B. Thank you.

CHAPTER 10 TEST

Page T46, Section E

Read and listen to the questions.

37. Where is the 1-bedroom apartment?
38. How much is the rent on the 2-bedroom unit?
39. Which pets are allowed in the building?
40. How much is the security deposit on the 1-bedroom apartment?

Now listen to the telephone conversation, and answer the questions.

A. City Square Apartments. May I help you?
B. Yes. Do you have any apartments available?

A. Yes, we do. We currently have two apartments available. We have a one-bedroom unit on the fifth floor, and we have a two-bedroom unit on the sixth floor.
B. I see. And how much is the rent?
A. The apartment on the sixth floor is $1,100 per month. The one-bedroom rents for $800 per month.
B. Is there a security deposit?
A. Yes. A deposit of two months rent is required when you sign the lease.
B. Are pets allowed in the building?
A. Cats and smaller pets are allowed, but not dogs.
B. And is there an elevator in the building?
A. Yes. There are two. Would you like to make an appointment to see the units?
B. Yes, please.

CHAPTER 11 TEST

Page T50, Section I

Read and listen to the questions.

38. When did she hurt her back?
39. Where did she hurt it?
40. What time does she have to be at the clinic?

Now listen to the conversation, and answer the questions.

A. Midtown Clinic.
B. Hello. I'd like to make an appointment, please.
A. What seems to be the problem?
B. I have a very bad backache.
A. I see. And when did your back begin to hurt?
B. Last Tuesday. I hurt it while I was moving some heavy boxes in the supply room at work.
A. Can you come in on Thursday morning at 7:30?
B. 7:30? Yes.
A. What's the name?
B. Veronica Matthews.
A. Telephone number?
B. (916) 728-9236.
A. Do you have medical insurance?
B. Yes.
A. And will this be your first visit to the Midtown Clinic?
B. Yes, it will.
A. Then please plan to arrive for your appointment fifteen minutes early to fill out a medical history form.

B. Fifteen minutes early? All right.
A. We'll see you on Thursday, Ms. Matthews.
B. Thank you.

CHAPTER 12 TEST

Page T54, Section G

Read and listen to the questions.

37. When does the book club meet?
38. How many evening programs are there each month?
39. How many hours is the library open on Wednesdays?
40. On which date will the children's story hour meet?

Now listen to the library's recorded announcements, and answer the questions.

This is the Central Library community events line. Here is the current listing of community events at the library. On the first Saturday of each month at 9 AM, children ages four to ten are invited to our children's story hour. On the third Thursday of each month, join librarian Kate Winters for the lunchtime book club. It meets in the community room at twelve noon. On the second and fourth Tuesdays of each month, come to our evening programs to learn about new books in the library collection. The programs start at 7:30. The Central Library is open Monday through Friday from 9 AM to 9 PM, Saturday from 9 AM to 6 PM, and Sunday from 1PM to 5 PM. Thank you for calling the Central Library community events line. Have a good day.

CHAPTER 13 TEST

Page T57, Section E

Read and listen to the questions.

35. Marina wants to fly from Los Angeles to Madrid, Spain. Which key should she press?
36. Roger wants to fly from Houston to Miami. Which key should he press?
37. Grace wants to make flight and hotel reservations for a tour of Italy. Which key should she press?
38. Daniel is looking for a job as a flight attendant. Which key should he press?
39. Karen didn't hear the first two instructions. Which key should she press?
40. Joseph is going to fly to New York tonight. Will his plane leave on time? Which key should he press?

Now listen to the telephone instructions, and answer the questions.

Thank you for calling National Airlines. Please make your selection from the following menu. For automated flight departure and arrival information, press 1. For travel reservations within the United States, press 2. For international travel reservations, press 3. For vacation packages, press 4. For all other information, press 5. To repeat this menu, press the star key.

a e i o u

حروف صدادار (؟) vowels

حروف بی صدا (؟) consanants

c b d ...

good   better   best
bad   worse   worst
little   less   least
much   more   most
far   farther/farther   farthest/farthest